MW01602782

Ah, Love! Let's thou and I with fate conspire
To grasp this sorry scheme of things entire,
Would not we shatter it to bits – and then
Re-mould it nearer to the heart's desire!

Omar Khayyam

Knowing others is wisdom;
Knowing the self is Enlightenment.
Mastering others requires force;
Mastering the self needs strength.

He who knows he has enough is rich.
Perseverance is a sign of willpower.
He, who stays where he is, endures.
To die but not to perish is to be eternally present.*

Lao Tsu in *Tao Te Ching*

To be eternally present... in the minds of the generations to come. The Tao is the supreme wisdom of the Infinite Intelligence. It accepts all life, but it does not profess reincarnation, afterlife, a religious God or any other religious creation of man.

Live each present moment completely and the future will take care of itself.
Fully enjoy the wonder and beauty of each instant.

Introduction

The lack of the *True Knowledge* prevents people from recognizing the true method, turning them into frustrated life-long seekers.

In 1953, Lester Levenson made an incredible discovery, but it was unintentionally concealed for decades behind the Releasing Technique. I have discovered it only recently – *The Transformation Process* – a simple and powerful method that Lester employed to realize Love and Freedom in three months.

"You can have, be, and do whatever you will or desire," says Lester.
"The only thing is stopping you is the accumulation of negative thoughts and feelings, which you are subconsciously holding.
"Remove these, and you remove the blocks to your accomplishing whatever you wish in life.

Live each present moment completely and the future will take care of itself. Fully enjoy the wonder and beauty of each instant.

Here Lester is giving us the *Transformation* – a Supreme Releasing process that brought him Love and Freedom. Only Classic meditation and *Transformation* will empower you to *have, be, and do whatever you will or desire*. Only these two methods will clean the subconscious of the hidden negativity and elevate you into the realm of Love where you will enjoy the fruits of *The Law of Happiness and Success* (explained later in the book). Releasing technique will help you to make temporary daily changes. It cannot eliminate the negative roots and transform you into a loving person. It cannot bring Happiness, only the *Transformation* or Classic meditation will.

An enlightened person can teach *Transformation* effectively. Lester did not want to be a teacher. "I never saw myself as a teacher." He said in Autobiography, "And I have no wish to start anything like a new movement. People were pulling on me, and I was giving because they were pulling." After proving the method, Lester suggested for the seekers to become teachers themselves. Lester's technique of *Transformation* is explained in depth in this book so that you could do it all by yourself.

My loving upbringing and meditation experience, as well as my experience with Lester, led me to recognize the value and benefits of the *Transformation process* that gifted Lester with Love and Freedom.

Both methods *Transformation* and Classic meditation have a common ingredient: *Witnessing the mind* (explained later in the book in the chapter *Realizing the*

Live each present moment completely and the future will take care of itself.
Fully enjoy the wonder and beauty of each instant.

Heart of Success: Transformation). The realization of Love takes place in both methods. After mastering *witnessing the mind* and unconditionally falling in love with ourselves, we would be able to engage the *Transformation process* effectively and realize Love, even experience Samadhi.

Most seekers do not find Happiness because they do not take care of their minds. There are always other priorities. Lacking *the Right Knowledge* the limited mind is making everything else more important except your Happiness. Most people never admit it. Look at yourself: where are you in life? Are you still seeking and riding the infamous rollercoaster called misery – a bit of satisfaction and back to misery?

The society created two industries intended to help people to Happiness and Success: spiritual industry and success industry. Unfortunately, both industries happened to be but moneymaking business, a hoax that corrupted the meaning of true Happiness and Success. Do you believe money and recognition will gift you with true Happiness and Success? Money is important, but it brings only temporary satisfaction. There is almost nothing real in dreamland when it comes to Happiness and Success. The only "real" thing there is success alternating with misery or no success at all.

The success industry defines the notion of success based on the erroneous values. Millions are listening anxiously to this unintentional deception with a hope of learning something. They learn nothing and spend the rest of their lives in a hopeless hope because they are taught how to become successful without any consideration given to Love and Talent. The true Happiness and Success are absent with spiritual and success industry teachers because they are bereft of the *Right Knowledge.*

When young and inexperienced, people believe what they have been taught: be a good citizen and a good student, work hard, and you will find success and happiness. These are empty words, a fairytale because to be truly Happy and Successful you must have the most important of all ingredients: (true) Love. With Love, you will discover your Talent and become Successful in the field corresponding to your talent.

"The only thing stopping you is the accumulation of negative thoughts and feelings, which you are subconsciously holding." What do you do about that? Maybe you did not experience negative events, thoughts, and feelings in the past? Maybe your subconscious is crisp and clear and has no negativity hidden in it? If that is true, you must have found true Happiness and Success long ago. You did not. Only with the realization of Love, you will experience an inexplicable joy of a life of (true) Happiness and Success. Wake up and see that you have been chasing shadows.

When we intentionally transform into Love the negative past that is locked in our subconscious, Love with a capital 'L' takes up residence in our heart. In that infinite moment we realize lasting Happiness and true Success.

Live each present moment completely and the future will take care of itself.
Fully enjoy the wonder and beauty of each instant.

Suddenly, all doors open.

It is not man's greatness, as it is perceived by others that matter most to the man himself, nor his achievements. Every U. S. president is looked upon as a great achiever. Henry Ford, J. P. Morgan, J. D. Rockefeller and their like are believed to be great achievers. In the absence of Love, true Happiness eluded these men. In the end, only true Happiness matters to a man himself and Love.

True Happiness (Happiness with a capital 'H') is a permanent peaceful state where the mind is free from negativity, and true Love (Love with a capital 'L') is the leader.

True Love is loving-kindness, compassion, understanding, and acceptance. It is our essence and is at the root of every human experience of love.

When achievement is rooted in Love, it is called true Success (Success with capital "S").

An occupation, no matter how enjoyable, will not result in Happiness; it can bring only temporary satisfaction. It is the same with your family. Only Love creates the result of Happiness that makes for the joy of occupation, the family everlasting, and all other joys.

When Love is absent, no accomplishment, regardless of its size, can bring Happiness. Like sex, achievements can bring only temporary satisfaction. (True) Success is incomparably more satisfying as it is beneficial to both, people and creator of Success. True Success is giving; it is shared. When created without Love, success is selfish; usually, only the business owners enjoy it.

"Living is giving. I won't deprive my family of knowing how good it feels to help those in need with some of the basics we already have…food, shelter, care and a future."

John Paul DeJoria, *The Giving People*

"There is nothing more satisfying and exciting than being able to affect people and noble causes in this world positively."

Dan Gilbert, *The Giving People*

Honoré De Balzac once said that behind every great wealth there is always a crime.

In the nineteenth century, a great phenomenon took place: Andrew Carnegie, a business tycoon who was brought up in a loving environment and led by Love. Carnegie's unparalleled example proved that great wealth can be created without crime and greed behind it and what is most important – the whole of it can be given back to people. Carnegie proved that an enormously successful business could be created with Love. He also demonstrated that when Love leads business, it brings Happiness to its owner.

When every child is raised in a loving environment, there will be Heaven on Earth because when a child is raised with Love, there will be almost no negativity in the child's subconscious, which would make it much easier for the child to gain Happiness and Success.

As a child, Stalin, the Soviet Dictator, grew up in a very poor family of the Georgian cobbler. Stalin's drunk father often beat him and his mother. Josef grew to become an angry liar, a pretender and a bandit with a criminal record. Hitler was a very bright child and was popular in school, but often clashed with his father over his interest in fine arts. It led to Hitler's detachment from his family, and he became a reclusive, discontented, resentful child, with an unstable temperament.

Nikolay's angry father who habitually raised a hand on his wife often was beating Nikolay. When the boy grew up and got married, the same pattern of the beating had continued in his family. Nikolay's son and daughter grew up in an unhealthy environment. When Nikolay came to America, he also invited his daughter to come over. Natasha fell in love with the US. Bright and beautiful, in a few years she became a successful realtor yet, her personal life went sour because she was a selfish and greedy person.

Natasha wanted to have family and children. She also wanted a wealthy husband. Now, twelve years later she is 35 and is still not married. Natasha's relationship with her father went down the drain so badly that Nikolay has confessed to me he has no daughter anymore. Driven by the hidden subconscious negativity this pattern of the sour relationships continue from generation to generation. It can be effectively brocken, however, when both Nikolay

Live each present moment completely and the future will take care of itself. Fully enjoy the wonder and beauty of each instant.

and Natasha would cleanse their subconscious from negativity.

It is amazing to watch how people are trying to repair their relationships without any consideration given to the negative past hidden in the subconscious. It is an impossible task to find Happiness and Success unless the negative past is transformed into Love. The mind fails you all the time, Love never will.

When raised with Love, it leads people to embrace naturally the idea of sharing and helping others as it is in the case of *The Giving People*. Those who grew up without Love are as naturally reject the idea of sharing and helping others because ignorance prevails in mind influenced by the negative subconscious past. The overwhelming majority of Americans are not raised in a loving environment. These people are not led by Love, which is the main reason for chaos in personal lives and life of humanity.

Have you been brought up with Love? If yes, you may use this book to confirm your good fortune with examples of the ordinary people and famous personalities who found Happiness and Success. As there is no limit to the inner refinement, you also may capitalize on some ideas in the book to accelerate it.

Live each present moment completely and the future will take care of itself.
Fully enjoy the wonder and beauty of each instant.

Sunrise at the ancient Lake Quaroun, Egypt

Realizing the Heart of Success

Transformation

You have captured the essence. This chapter is a beautiful testimony to the power of Love. I think for each of us, the path is the same, yet different. But people like you are beacons who, simply by example, embody the potential of living life from another higher perspective. In the language of the Course of Miracles, you are a "miracle-worker." "Miracles" are their word for changes in perception - the path from fear to love.

I believe the Course of Miracles is a sacred text. I also feel that your teaching might prove to make its message more accessible to the thousands of people who read it, are captured by its power, yet find it hard actually to practice. It could be a world-changing message, yet it needs people like you - who already live its principles - to help spread the message of the transformational power of Love.   Jim Nowak

In a democratic society, people erroneously believe they are free. In reality, the society effectively exercises control over your inner world from outside. If you want to have your own life, you need to learn how to control your outer world from inside.

In fact, you already have a life of Happiness and Success but only at the level that you set up so far, unaware. This chapter will explain how to eliminate the negative subconscious influence and find what you are looking for.

Following is a letter from the reader:

Yuri,

Thank you for this book... It is so clear to me. You have helped me close the final chapter of my search for what Lester had discovered.

I bought four whole Sedona method programs as well as supplementary courses... it took me all this to find the truth in these programs, audios, and CDs...all be it small pieces.

However, once you put them together and stand back one can only realize that Lester went free without using the method (Ed. Releasing).

I did leave a 5-star review for your book.... (Radical D)...Thank you from the bottom of my heart you have brought to the surface a long-buried secret of Lester's freedom. I feel like I am free already.

I will be eternally grateful to you. This book is the answer. Reading the Transformation chapter, I was screaming Yes yes yes! To myself as the words played out and led me the way to freedom. I plan to scrutinize your book and read many times, as I did that pdf.

Much love to you!!!

Take care!!!

Recently, I asked some people "What is the Heart of (true) Success?" Many thought it was hard work; others named perseverance, confidence, even connections, some believe "luck" is at the Heart of Success... Whether religious believers or not, people do not know (true) Love.

In his work, *The Republic*, the Greek philosopher Plato (c.429-347 BC) employed the allegory of a cave to describe the human condition of *resistance*. This allegory – in which humans live imprisoned in a dark cave, deep underground – is the perfect metaphor for having to live in a state of no Love.

Because people are in constant change, they are capable of the most astonishing *Transformation*. *Transformation* of one's negative past into Love is the most rewarding example of such change. Love is inexplicably a wonderful and powerful state of being. Is there any other state, anything that can be compared to the state of Love? Just imagine yourself to experience only Love, the amazing stae of Love all the time

When Love is absent, there is still some goodness remaining, says the Tao, humanity's well of wisdom.

When goodness is gone, morality comes up. When morality is no longer present, rituals come up, which is the beginning of chaos.

Love is the radiance and the extension of Infinite Intelligence in the human world. This unusual, mysterious, inexplicable state brings Happiness and transforms a human being into a Human Being.

Like water, Love is effortlessly nourishing all things. Thoughts weaken the mind; desires wither hearts. When we open ourselves to Love, the mind falls quiet and follows Love's lead. Open yourself to Love and trust yourself, your intuition, which is the voice of Love.

Every true saint was a loving person. Regardless of their chosen path, every one of them became free by first realizing Love. How did they do it?

Their confidence is the key.

It makes no difference what one chooses to put his confidence in. The strength of the confidence makes all the difference because the strength of the confidence enables one to transcend the ego. It may be a symbol of God, Life, Infinite Intelligence, or Universe. Symbols do not make any difference since symbols are principles and principles are dead. A dead principle or symbol cannot help transcend egotism. Total confidence in symbol does it, confidence that is stronger than our life-long confidence in mind.

Unshakable confidence in a crocodile, a tree or your Self will do the same job as unshakable confidence in God or deity. Religion wants people to rely on outside means. However, every human imperfection is superficial and may be correct by the man himself. It is insane to transfer

Live each present moment completely and the future will take care of itself. Fully enjoy the wonder and beauty of each instant.

your innate ability to command your life to some entity or the bunch of bones unless your confidence in this entity or bones beyond the shadow of the doubt.

Confidence in Love, however, is our best choice. Whether it is business or relationships, the finest part of you, Love, is your best adviser.

When we transform our past into Love, negativity is gone, and mind's limitations dissolve. The mind becomes obedient, and Love intuitively lights our way. The limited mind will never believe it ahead of time and will build barriers of resistance in your path. As you keep transforming your past into Love, Love will be more often your leader. The less negativity remains in the subconscious, the higher we fly, as we drop the heaviest load of all, the ego, which is the mind's limitations.

There is nothing that can be done without the mind. If you wish to go beyond the limitations of your mind, you must start by making your limited mind your best friend. Lester's mind was already his best friend. However, when oblivious to his condition, Lester started his intense search (where *intense* means *concentrated*), for 30 days his mind was not able to find the answers. Nevertheless, his mind brought him to a threshold, from where answers had become possible.

How did it happen?

When, at 43, Lester had a deadly heart attack, the doctor told him that he might drop dead at any time. Facing his dire condition, Lester decided either he will find the answers to What is life? What is it all about? Is there a reason for my being here in this world, and if so, what is it? or take his life. He started with reading books, but in four days, it hit him that if the answers could be found somewhere in an outside world, he surely would have found them long ago since these questions had plagued him all his life. Suddenly, he saw it: the problems lie within; therefore, the answers must also be within. From that time on, his search became extremely intense.

At the end of the first month, he stumbled upon something very important, probably the most important of all questions: What is *Happiness*? Within several days of intense trial and error, Lester had his answer: Happiness is when I love the other one, which means Happiness is a feeling within me. If that is so, he thought, even if I cannot change my unhappy past, I could change how I *felt* about one situation or another. I could transform it into Love, which equals Happiness. That was an incredible discovery! It made him feel certain he was in the driver's seat because he could now change to Love whatever non-loving feeling he had felt in the past.

A Happiness is synonymous with Love and is beyond common sense, it is beyond logic, beyond our limited mind. However, all of this helps us realize Love. Lester was using logic, reason, and common sense; he was intensely using his mind. Lester's intensity helped to accelerate his search. He had no distractions; he turned off his phone and TV; he was no longer concerned with his illness, even death. Such an incredibly intense search also had exhausted his emotional thinking process.

When Lester's mind finally gave up and fell quiet, Lester was able to hear the voice of Love. The more extreme the intensity of the process, the sooner mind falls quiet, and the higher becomes the probability of receiving an intuitive answer. Isolation creates a kind of spiritual spa because it filters out all distractions.

Lester was searching for answers in the dark. He accidentally stumbled upon the *Transformation process,* which is now available to use without initial search.

One who is aware makes good use of his aloneness because he intuitively knows it is a shorter path to realization of Love.

Why would people isolate themselves in deserts, in forests? They had no methods, but intuitively they knew that isolation would help them find God. In reality, they were looking for peace and Happiness, which they thought they would receive from God. Indeed, they knew the present could not be properly understood without exploring the past.

Lester isolated himself for three months from the world and people he loved and that allowed him an intense concentration. Nevertheless, from the moment he discovered he could transform his past into Love, it took Lester only one month to realize Love. Lester was searching in the dark, yet we have a proven method. Depending on your determination and intensity, it may take you longer than one month to realize Love, but it will happen. It cannot be any other way.

At the same time, Lester realized that he was responsible for everything that happened to him because it all happened as result of his haphazard emotional-thinking process and subconscious negativity. All these realizations resulted from the process of logical trial and error and brought Lester to the most important step.

 His entire life came up for a review as he decided to transform into Love his entire past, all past hurts, and disappointments. Today, psychologists are well aware of the tremendous influence of the subconscious past.

Lester says, discovering that my Happiness equated to my loving and that my thinking was the cause of things happening to me in my life gave me more and more freedom; freedom from the subconscious compulsions that I had to work, I had to make money, I had to have girlfriends. Freedom in the feeling that I was now able to determine my destiny, I was now able to control my world, lightened my internal burden so strongly that I felt there was no need for me to have to do anything. Plus, this Happiness was so great. It was a new experience for me. I was experiencing a joy that I never knew existed, never dreamed could be. So I decided, "This is so great, I'm not going to stop until I carry it all the way." I had no idea how far it could go. I had no idea how joyous a person could be. But I was determined to find out.

In Lester's example, the uniqueness lies in his irrevocable decision, perseverance, and intensity, all of which had intensified when Lester isolated himself. All of these put Lester on the supreme path of Love.

Lester says, "When I mixed with people, and again and again when they would do things that I didn't like and within me was a feeling of non-Love, I would immediately change that attitude to one of loving. Eventually, I got to a point where, no matter how much I was opposed, I could feel only Love."

20

Live each present moment completely and the future will take care of itself.
Fully enjoy the wonder and beauty of each instant.

As Lester was transforming his past, he also shed his desires. When we reach a certain point in the process of transforming negativity to Love when we realize that Love is real, that Love is such a beneficial and powerful force, we simply let Love shine and evaporate every bit of negativity, and every desire that is not rooted in Love.

Lester was pushed with his back against the wall. He was under the gun: he was nearly dead, but he did not try to heal his body. It is very important to understand. He made an Irrevocable Decision to find the answers. He started by healing his mind. When Love healed his mind, his body also was healed, as if by itself.

"I began to feel stronger as the weight of my pain dropped away. I was happier than I had ever been before, and I kept it going…"

For Happiness, we move within. Any other goal may temporary sidetrack us by taking into an opposite direction: without. In that, we are making our choice: Happiness, and nothing else. As to your goal of Happiness and Success, it will benefit you tenfold when you first find Happiness because Love will become your guide and you will swiftly accomplish the Success part of your goal.

There are countless triggers of irritation within and all around us, and there are many hidden reasons. We may try hard to convince ourselves not to be irritable; we may use affirmations, releasing. These are helpful but temporary measures. Irritation will persist because it is nearly impossible to pinpoint its deeply buried cause(s). Only when you transform your past into Love there will be no more irritation and a trigger; any trigger will become powerless.

Live each present moment completely and the future will take care of itself.
Fully enjoy the wonder and beauty of each instant.

In *Transformation*, vividly imagine an event you are transforming. *Imagination* would greatly enhance the process. For example, imagine loving something you do not like. Transform to Love to that "thing" every negative emotion and thought all pros and cons and, at that moment, you will be moved into the world of Love that knows no negativity.

An affirmation can be your aid. There is a good example of affirmations used by John D. Rockefeller's "I am bound to be rich!" and "I am bound to live 100 years!" Despite ailing during the first half of his life, Rockefeller fulfilled both of his wishes. However, you would need Rockefeller's conviction and determination to obtain a similar effect. As it is with a *Talent*, it is impossible to measure another's determination, intensity, and conviction. Your best bet would be to note the other people's examples but create your own affirmation rooted in Love. The affirmation also helps to stop mind's wondering and keep it focused on the task.

There are many beautiful mantras on Utube.com. I do not use it as I enjoy peace more than anything else.

When uneducated, the mind is not interested in transforming the past misfortunes into Love. It loves to talk about Love; it loves to read about Love. We may spend life collecting information about Love from scriptures, teachings, and novels. We may become an encyclopedia of Love and still not know Love. The mind will know everything about Love and will even think that it loves with true Love. But, something will happen, and at once, the mind will forget about Love, irritation will happen, anger will happen.

The mind loves to talk about the past; it loves to think about past success, memorable vacations, and other happy moments. Hurts and frustrations… the mind does not want to think about the past sorrows, it wants to forget it, and it is successful in forgetting and entombing it deep inside. Oh no! Not again! Immediately the Resistance is on.

When transforming negativity into Love, from your earliest childhood, one by one bring to the light of the present each negative memory of distant events and perform the magic of *Transformation.* You will soon notice how this process will begin changing your attitude, your moods, your behavior. You will come to appreciate this gift and will encourage your mind to continue until you complete the *Transformation* process. You may use pictures or list of memories, events, starting from the time you remember yourself. Family albums may be used, or you may simply retrospect on your past. See if you could come up with your idea of an aid.

Use comparison. For example, relate negativity to a mirage in a desert. In a desert, the mirage produces an incredible display of images. If we do not recognize the mirage as an illusion, we fall under its spell, and these ever-changing ephemeral images will mislead us in our travel. Once we see it for what it is, its influence evaporates.

It is the same with negativity and Love. When it is conditioned, not loving, the mind believes the negativity is an inseparable part of life. It is true for a dreamland but not in the world of Love. When the mind is dreaming, its conviction empowers negativity's influence, making people fall deeper under its spell. The ever-changing non-loving feelings and thoughts are forever misleading them in their journey. *Transformation* of the subconscious negativity into Love dissolves negative influence. As soon as we understand it, our vision clears, and we see that in the light of Love negativity's influence evaporates like the mirage in the desert and like the mirage, it loses its power over us.

Suffering is not imagined, war and murder are real whether Love is realized or not. This negativity can exert a very powerful influence only on the minds that do not know Love. The same negativity is powerless against a mind led by Love.

There are two kinds of negativity: internal and external. With releasing, we can let go of the internal negative influence but only partially. The *Transformation* will eliminate nearly all of it and will "elevate" us into the dimension of Love. *The Momentum of Love* (see below) will ensure completion of the process despite our not remembering some negative events of the past.

As to the external negativity, *Transformation* renders its influence powerless because when is led by Love the mind becomes a witness. A true witness is beyond the negative influence. Indeed, it is another dimension, and when we are there, we leave this dreamland's influence behind. From there, the mind sees through people and events of the dreamland. With the realization of Love, our mind indeed becomes an impartial witness, compassionate, and understanding.

A dreamland is an individual environment created unaware, usually without Love. It is but a pile of concepts, ideas, thoughts, and feelings, as well as an archive containing our every experience.

Why things beautiful often carry with them a touch of sadness? Because this too shall pass☺ There will be more beautiful things in your life, but it too will pass. Love yourself. Watch your mind and transform your negative past into Love so that the beauty of Love and Life is yours forever, that you could enjoy each present moment completely.

Surround yourself with things uplifting, simple, and nice. There needs to be nothing negative in your environment.

Smile

An aid to the *Transformation process* will be more effective when it is used intensely – charged with mental energy. The stronger is the charge (unabstracted concentration) the higher is the intensity of the process.

Smile! No matter how difficult is the situation you are transforming, smile. Smile is magic. It brings with it mystery of relaxation. People usually do not smile when they are dealing with difficulties. However, sincere smile is the sister of Love. A smile is a powerful means to disable your Resistance program and rise above mental conditioning.

Smile at near stupidity of the situation when ten years after falling apart you still hate your former partner. You know you are causing damage to your health with this negative influence but cannot stop hating whenever you remember this relationship. Smile! Force a smile!

Instantly you will discover you are in a squirrel cage, hating, and then trying to convince yourself you are indifferent. Then back to hating, then – trying to forget, then hating yourself for doing something wrong, and so on, Smile! Instantly your attitude will change, and the *Transformation process* will become an easy process.

A smile is an immensely powerful tool. When in the heat of rage you suddenly stop and smile (at yourself, at the silliness of the situation, at the circus you believed was the life you were living so far). Instantly, you are free☺

Time heals, and this seems to be true but only to the degree. Past emotions are easier to deal with as their impact becomes weaker with time. Unfortunately, time eliminates neither emotions nor their causes. With a closer look, we recognize that time can only "dress the wound" but not heal it. Love heals.

Transformation

The ignorant mind fails to recognize its subconscious influence.

Transformation requires a full mind's cooperation, which happens when our mind gets educated with the *Right knowledge*. An educated mind's strength lies in its unwavering confidence in the unmatched benevolent power of Love. Anyone can realize Love. What we then accomplish with Love is truly wonderful, almost magical. To experience this magic, we have to become loving magicians.

Live each present moment completely and the future will take care of itself. Fully enjoy the wonder and beauty of each instant.

Indeed, some magical elements are present in the process of realization of Love. With the realization of Love, we come close to the state of Freedom, a truly magical state.

The Momentum of Love is another magic. When we are sincerely doing all we can at transforming our negative past into Love, we are literary moved to the end of the *Transformation* process with the *Momentum of Love* (explained below) which finalizes it with no more effort on our part.

One of the difficulties in the process of *Transformation* lies in our subconscious confusion of the meaning of true Love with a common understanding of love to parents, boyfriend, child, etc.

When we are about to transform into Love negative feelings for someone we do not like, immediately resistance surges and we say something like "He is a weather-beaten rat! How could I love this person?" It happens because our subconscious is constantly influencing our emotional thinking process. In this particular case, it is confusing us into using a common meaning of love instead of Love, which is compassion and understanding.

There is only one Love: the state of Love to which people attribute/create numberless shades. They are numberless because in every situation everyone's mind creates its shade of Love congruent with the qualities of the creator. As you keep transforming your past into Love these shades disappear....

Live each present moment completely and the future will take care of itself.
Fully enjoy the wonder and beauty of each instant.

There is no direct connection between the limited mind and Love. Love is beyond the mind's limitations (beyond ignorance); it is state of the intuitive knowing. When the mind's limitations dissolve, Love shines, and there is no need for connection because the mind is now loving. Love is a changeless boundless power of the highest good. Love is an inseparable part of ourselves, but the limitations of the mind you acquired. The mind's ETP (Emotional Thinking Process) and the negative subconscious past obscure Love yet, *Transformation* can be done only with the mind's cooperation. Unwavering decision to transform your negative past into Love will establish such cooperation.

You may transform negativity directly into Love, or you may use one of Love's attributes: acceptance, understanding, compassion, and kindness. You may also use releasing to aid *Transformation* process.

Surround yourself with things nice, uplifting, and simple. There must be no negativity in your environment. Create your mantra as an aid to *Transformation*. Music may not be necessary. It can be just a short fraise or a poem. Omar Khayyam's little poems translated by Fitzgerald present a great choice of an aid.

That spring should vanish with the rose.
That youth's sweet-scented manuscript
 should close.
The Nightingale that in the branches sang,
Whence and whither flown again, who knows.

Chose what is most appealing to you. When you get stuck, when you are frustrated, smile and employ your mantra for a couple of minutes; it will bestow encouragement upon you. Then, go back and *transform* that difficult situation. Work with nostalgia as it inherently infused with sadness that you need to transform into Love.

You may also use Rule of the Lost Keys. In this case scenario, patience is the key. When keys are misplaced, and you cannot find it what is the best thing to do? Leave it alone, knowing it will surface. You may employ the same method in the *Transformation process.* Some tough past negative event may be getting stubborn when you would try to transform it into Love. After a sincere but unsuccessful attempt to transform it into Love, leave it alone, knowing it is already resolved, that the key is already found on the mental plain. Get busy with another event and lo at the moment the least expected, you will be compelled to come back to the stubborn one and *transform* it into Love with ease.

Do not try to figure it out how you can love someone who "doesn't deserve" it. Do not try to "figure out" anything. The mind loves figuring things out, most of the time unsuccessfully. Instead, use Love's point of view.

Throughout the *Transformation* process, keep in mind a simple thought: "The *Transformation* is propelling me into a life of Happiness and Success" (modify it to your liking). Do not analyze this thought; keep it in the back of your mind.

It seems impossible to love someone you hate. Here is Lester's approach to Dr. Schulz: "<u>The point is not whether he deserves love. The point is can you do it? Is it possible to simply change a feeling of hatred into a feeling of love – not for the benefit of the other person but for yourself?</u>" It is an excellent example of logic and common sense. Contemplate it as you begin your *Transformation process*: there is much power to it.

Keep this approach in mind throughout the entire process: you Love not for the benefit of another person, but first, for your benefit. You will be able to benefit many people when you *transform* your past into Love.

These powerful lines will enable you instantly transform almost every negativity. When you have difficulties, apply acceptance and understanding. Imagine looking into that person's eyes. If associated negative emotions come up, let it go and let perfection be, knowing Love is perfection. Remember: you are doing it for your benefit.

Lester's suggestion is powerful and direct. Always try it first. There are no two situations or people alike. Dr. Schulz's was not a negative event; it was made negative by Lester's anger, which blinded him. Bush Jr. may be a much more complicated negative situation where he caused hundreds of thousands civilian deaths; American soldiers killed and wounded; the collapse of the US economy; endorsement of torture; and so on. This man is much harder to deal with than with Dr. Schulz.

It would be against our nature to love people like Bush, Cheney, Lenin, and Hitler and it is not necessary. Transform into Love for humanity and life every negative emotion associated with this kind of people and events. Indifference is a cover for a deeply hidden negative attitude. If we have negative feelings towards any person – we are not in the state of Love.

When Love is realized, it celebrates the death of all negativity. A (true) Love is not an emotion; it is expressed through its properties of understanding, acceptance, compassion, and kindness. When it comes to deeply negative situations, do not use the word love, instead, utilize Love's properties.

When your past is *transformed* into Love, what is left? At that point you will not be able to experience negative emotions no matter what kind of person or event you are facing, Stalin, Bush or Hitler, for you will be forever anchored in a peaceful state of Love. Though it is not an unencumbered peace of Freedom, it is peaceful enough to make you a witness that sees clearly through people and events.

You will not love a murderer but without any negativity left within you what will be your attitude towards this kind of people? Certainly not hate, irritation or indifference, then what it will be? A right attitude. A state of the realized Love is a very personal and hardly describable, yet you will appreciate and enjoy this state – the best place to be in. You always will have this right loving attitude. You would prove yourself Love as the answer.

31

Live each present moment completely and the future will take care of itself. Fully enjoy the wonder and beauty of each instant.

The Momentum of Love

We cannot transform 100% of the past into Love, as we do not remember many past events. However, there is *The Momentum of Love* that is enforced when we have earnestly transformed everything we remember. At that moment, the force of Love overwhelms the unremembered part of the subconscious past and burns off the rest of the negativity, thus instantly making *Transformation* process complete. The timing cannot be determined as it depends on individual factors.

Lester mention, when we release all we can, the rest is completed on its own. Interestingly, *The Momentum of Love* also is ruling enlightenment in meditation: after many a hundred hours of intense meditation, suddenly, happens Samadhi that banishes all remaining negativity together with the influence of all remaining concepts. It "lifts" one beyond the conscious and subconscious mind into an unknown, indescribable state where the magic of meditation is instantly completed. Whether it is Samadhi or *Transformation*, the shock of completion is so powerful it will "keep" one immersed in the state of Love for the rest of life.

Transformation is a creative process. As in meditation, we must learn how to be our masters. Disciplene, persistence, and intense practice would do the job.

Fully enjoy the wonder and beauty of each instant, and the future will take care of itself. As you enjoy each present moment completely, transform into Love anything that is not that joy, and you may get into the world of Love this way.

Lester's example with Dr. Schulz is encouraging.

"First," he asked himself, "was I experiencing a lack of love that day?"

"Yes," he answered aloud. "Nobody gave a damn about me, not the nurses, not the orderlies, not even Dr. Schultz. They did not care. As sick as I was, they threw me out, sent me home to die so they would not have to watch one of their failures. Well, the hell with them. They can all go to hell." He was shocked at the vehemence in his voice. His body trembled with rage, and he felt weak. He hated the doctor. He could feel it burning in his chest. "Oh, boy," he thought," this sure isn't love."

"Well, can I change it?" he asked. "Is it possible to turn it into love for the doctor?"

"Hell, no," he thought, "Why should I? What did he ever do to deserve any love?"

"That's not the point," he answered himself. "The point is not whether he deserves love. The point is can you do it? Is it possible to change a feeling of hatred into a feeling of love – not for the benefit of the other person but for yourself?"

As the thought crossed his mind, he felt something break loose in his chest. A gentle easing, a sense of dissolving, and the burning sensation was gone. He did not trust it at first. It seemed too easy, so he pictured the scene again with Dr. Schultz in the hospital. He was surprised to find that it brought only a mild feeling of resentment rather than the previous intense burning hatred. He wondered if he could do it again.

"Let's see," he thought, "what did I just do? Ah, yes. Can I change this feeling of resentment into a feeling of love?" He chuckled as <u>he felt the resentment dissolve in his chest. Then it was gone, and he was happy.</u>

"Doctor Schultz, you son-of-a-gun," he said, grinning, "I love you."

It is a very important point: "<u>The point is not whether he deserves love. The point is can you do it? Is it possible to simply change a feeling of hatred into a feeling of love – not for the benefit of the other person but for yourself?</u>" Lester has discovered this deeply meaningful key. Make sure you grasp this meaning, which will make your sailing to Love much smoother.

It is impossible to get down to the cause of every negative emotion because the cause may have nothing to do with a current situation. It is possible you created the actual cause when you were only three years old. Not too many people would be able to remember what happened at that age. Simply remembering does not reach most of our very early experiences because we had them before we had language. A small child would have no idea of the cause of the pain, even less so it would be able to explain it. The older we become, the deeper these early negative memories are buried in the subconscious.

Year after year says Dr. Jack Lee Rosenberg in his book *Body, Self, Soul and Sustaining Integration*, the sealed-off irritant blocks the free flow of energy through the body and it may restrict the free range of feelings. The more painful the initial wound, the tighter is the muscular defense and the less it is accessible. Releasing cannot reach that far, but *Transformation* will. Our conscious effort of *Transformation* may not reach that deep either, yet *The Momentum of Love* will eradicate remaining negative causes.

When jealousy or anger overwhelms us, though not dealing with the cause, releasing would be most effective at this very moment of the flaming emotion. Did you ever try to release an overwhelming emotion at its peak? An impossible task. If you can do it, instantly you will be free. We always "forget" releasing when we are under the influence of the powerful negative feelings. We remember about releasing later and "later" releasing becomes not nearly as effective as at the time of rage.

However, even without having a sound witnessing experience, we can literary witness the past event and deal with corresponding emotions almost at arm's length. When these "past" emotions arise, they are usually not nearly as powerful as at the time of that distant event and are nearly not as powerful as those experienced in daily life. Thus, they are much easier to release via transforming them into Love.

Believe not because some old manuscripts are produced. Believe not because it is your national belief. Believe not because you have been made to believe from your childhood, but reason truth out, and after you have analyzed it, then if you find it will do good to one and all, believe it, live up to it and help others live up to it.

In the process of *Transformation* measure up negative situations against this quote to be convinced that all of them must be transformed into Love.

With the *Transformation* comes two benefits. We permanently eliminate hidden causes of negative emotions and lose the ability to become angry, greedy, fearful, apathetic, proud, and so on. It will all be gone together with irritation, annoyance and other negativity. Occasionally, we may still go off track and experience hints of some of these negative emotions. However, we can now instantly let them go – transform into Love and usually – at their root and before they fully manifest themselves.

When we realize Love, we are not yet free as Freedom means an unencumbered peace. However, Freedom is also a state of non-doing whether mentally or physically. This state comes closest to what we call Infinite Intelligence – an originator and sustainer of our universe and beyond. However, Infinite Intelligence' "non-doing" means doing absolutely everything but in ways yet inconceivable.
Unlike Infinite Intelligence, being in a state of Freedom we cannot originate or create anything. In the state of Freedom, we can only experience the unencumbered peace that entirely transforms our being. When we "step down" or come back to the dreamland we are able to think, imagine and create while being led by Love, which is the same state that we experience as the result of the *Transformation.*

As you move through your day, remember to *Live each present moment completely so that the future will take care of itself. Fully enjoy the wonder and beauty of each instant* and turn every thought that contradicts this statement into a loving thought, every feeling – into a loving feeling. As you do this, you will be elevated into the world of Love. Do not get discouraged if in the beginning you may forget to follow this route. A simple and persistent reminder could do a great deal of work if not magic. Gently remind yourself to continue and keep enjoying it. Place the notes/reminders with these lines around your place. When you get irritated or annoyed, it will instantly remind of Love and the importance of the enjoyment of each instant. Smile, and you are back on track, feeling loving again. To ensure the success of this practice, you must learn to watch your mind (explained below) and to love yourself.

The Lie of Principle
Adopted, with changes, from *The Lion Moves Alone*

When we do not have confidence in Love, in what is real, what is natural, we live by the made-up principles and artificial concepts. We live by what we have learned from parents, teachers, society, and religion. We have been taught to believe in principles.

A reader was complaining: "No one wants to be a friend with a guillotine." He is right: except for gravediggers, no one wants to handle corpses. He turned himself into a guillotine. His principle is to cut off the heads to all those who are not in agreement with his principles. It means cutting off many heads. To him, it does not matter. What matters is a principle. He is 50, and he will live for another 70 years. Does it make any sense? He is already dead: a guillotine, a piece of metal.

When we are not aware, we are nearly dead; we exist mechanically, existing with habits, dead concepts, and principles. It cannot be otherwise because when awareness is low, principle or concept becomes a ruler whether it is guillotine or kindness. If you are greedy, you could try to make yourself a kind person and kindness will become your principle but you will not become kindness. You would remain the same greedy person, but now your greed will be covered with a mask of kindness. Only when Love is realized you will become kindness and Love.

Misha landed in the US several years back. A year later, he invited his young daughter Masha, and she decided to stay in America. Soon, Masha became a successful young woman, but her relationship with father deteriorated. The two were close to me, and I was trying to have them talk, yet father refused to talk to his daughter because he wanted to be true to his principle: "When people betray me I cut them off forever, whether they are friends, children or relatives." Masha did not betray her father. There was unpleasant arguing a couple of times. After that, father refused to make the first call. He said he is indifferent to his daughter. However, there is no such thing as indifference, which is simply a cover for negative emotions (in this case sadness and frustration) we do not wish to face.

Society cultivates inferior people by making them adopt inappropriate principles. The Holy Inquisition of the Catholic Church that for 800 years was burning people alive in the name of God is a good example of how a principle can turn human beings into a bloody monster.

Roman popes had rarely attended these holy fires. The 'unfaithful', their children and wives have been burned alive by those who lived by the principles of the holy church, created by the ignorant human beings.

In school, we have been told of importance abiding the principles. We were taught supreme principles. Unfortunately, being an artificial creation of unaware minds, even supreme principles are dead weight. Make a note of how society describes this tool of control:

The principle is 1. The fundamental truth, law, a moving force that creates the basis for other truths, laws and moving forces. 2. A governing condition, main rule, the directive for any action. 3. Inner conviction, the point of view, the standard of behavior.

The above is mainly not true. The truth is substituted in a dreamland with blabber that confuse people. In the world of Love, there is no need for controls, there is no need for standards of behavior, laws, and rules. There is no need for moving forces either, as Love is the most powerful moving force and it is ours with the realization of Love.

Principles are created by the desire to assert. At the core of violence, there is always a principle that justifies it. Nothing exposes the nature of a principle better than its justification of violence. Principles are never truthful. There are many seem to be useful principles in dreamland. However, none of these principles will help you to wake up and move beyond the illusion of dreamland. It is one of many reasons why religion failed with all its dogmas/principles to help people to wake up. Every religion, including Eastern religion, was created not to liberate, but to control with principles that negate true Love.

In religion, Love is an empty word; it has no substance. Thus, religion is misleading. The religion itself is a principle conjured to dominate, separate and frighten with hallucinating, often sick concepts like Armageddon. Would Love create the Armageddon? The question itself is dumb☺ Such a fabrication could take place only in dreamland's quagmire. Believers accept this lie and adopt it. Imagine what a tremendous negative shock this principle would make on the believer's genetic makeup. Society lives by its principles but in nature, in the flow of life there is no need for principles, and we are an integral part of nature.

When living in the present, when you realize Love you can live in the society and be beyond its principles. Someone may say true Love is also a principle. It is true but only for the one who talks about Love; when one has realized Love, there is no more principles but a peaceful state of Love.

In the dreamland, the principle is made important. To the one who walks the road of Love and Freedom, there are no useful principles because every principle is a limitation. In the world of Love, words *belief* and *faith* lose their dreamland's significance.

Love and Freedom are unprincipled. Honesty and kindness are our nature. Ignorance manipulates principles; it divides by principles. It creates enemies with principles. 'Who is not with us, is against us.' If there were no enemy, this principle certainly would help to create one. American Democrats are the best bunch in the world at creating fake principles. Sleazy and inept, they created an enemy from Russia to take people's attention away from their fraud and damage they keep causing to the country. Like the selfish desire that is not rooted in Love, the principle impedes the way to Happiness; it undermines Love, for any principle is but masqueraded selfish desire.

Like Buddha, Jesus was unprincipled (if he was at all). Like any other true teacher, Jesus created no school, no organization, but the ignorant followers did not miss this opportunity. The followers created the whole system of principles called Christian Religion.

It happened so many times throughout history: enlightened teacher dies, the followers corrupt the teaching and create new religion.... and millenniums of suffering. When a selfish desire is at the root of creation, the result is always smeared with suffering, but when there is a canning desire, the result is as disastrous as 800 years of the Catholic Inquisition. To protect itself, ignorance builds prison bars of principles through which no Love can shine. Love is a life that carries everything in its stream, including religion. Ignorance fears Love because when exposed to the light of Love, ignorance evaporates.

Live each present moment completely and the future will take care of itself.
Fully enjoy the wonder and beauty of each instant.

Resistance

The following letter demonstrates how conditioning and resistance are tricking the mind into total denial. My comments are incorporated into the body of the letter with quotation marks.

Юрочка, here I am again, spilling my guts:

I realized not long time ago that my mind is my friend, including ego, which is kind of emotional counterpart of mind. Limited, but instrumental for every day. They served me all my life to the best of their abilities. When I start the day with pain in my heart and body, I question my mind. I know this is all in my head. Then I talk to it and then take care of daily chores. Sooner than later, I take a glass of wine. It is my anesthesia from pain. It is obvious that I am escaping pain inside of my being, which is as it is now...

"The ego is ephemeral and does not exist. There is no need for made up things like ego and soul in the process of *Transformation.* All we need is Love. Your mind failed to serve you right. If it served you right, you would not find yourself in this desperate state. To question your limited mind is useless. Questions reinforce resistance, ignorance. When Love is realized, it will provide you with an intuitive answer to your every question. As you can see, your mind cannot provide you with answers, yet it was successful in erroneously convincing you that vine would banish pain. As you can see, you are mistaken thinking that your mind is your friend. It will become your friend when despite all odds, convictions, excuses, laziness, and dead principles you educated it with *The Right Knowledge* that leads to *Transformation* or *Classic Meditation.*"

I am full of love to my husband and my ex – B. I take care of them. I love my friends and my former students, scattered all over the world. And my relatives. And I receive back a lot in return. Love.
Then, where the pain is nestling in me?

"The causes of your pain are hidden in your subconscious. Your love to relatives and friends is a shallow surface matter. It is shallow because it is powerless to give you peace and bestow true Happiness upon you. True Love encompasses all people and the universe."

I retrospect into my past: watch the movies in my memories about my parents, my sister, my most dramatic moments in life, like when I hung myself in a garage and was saved, many tears, scar on the neck from the rope, that lasted many years... etc. - and my heart is washed with Love and forgiveness to everyone and myself.

"This is mostly your wishful thinking for when our heart is washed with true Love; you would have no pain, no drinking, and no smoking. You would enjoy each present moment completely and let the future to take care of itself without a single thought of the past or future. When you realize Love, it becomes an integral part of your everyday life. It guides your every decision and makes it right whatever you do."

WHAT ELSE CAN I DO?

"If you wish to have a life, which means enjoyment of life's each moment, you must clean the subconscious of the past negativity; simple like that. There is no other way☺"

I gave myself an indulgence to use alcohol and cigarettes, these habits... yet, I forgive myself for it. At the same time, I have an underlying suspicion that I am destroying myself. It is obvious that my habits are not rooted in Love. (Because I used to think that loving means to be clean and sober... as I used to be for a while.)
It feels, as regardless of thousands of books, various practices and my deepest believes into the nature of life and universe - Love, that maybe I am not destined for Transformation.

"Drinking and smoking are caused by having no fulfillment and true Love. You have no fulfillment because your negative past sabotages your good intentions. Like everyone else, you are driven by your past while trying to forgive yourself. Your forgiveness of yourself is your mind's just another trick because if you truly forgive yourself and come to love yourself unconditionally, there will be no indulgences that are destroying you. Could you see how tricky the mind is? When there is a true Love, there is no space left for the damaging habits, anger, and moods."

I am so tired!!! Like this morning: I woke up so devastated, because of my dreams. I was jealous and heartbroken. And even though, I knew it came from harboring issues in my subconscious, it had overwhelming power on my awakened mind and body. I felt handicapped!

Live each present moment completely and the future will take care of itself. Fully enjoy the wonder and beauty of each instant.

"As you can see, your limited mind-friend cannot overcome your subconscious negative influence. It cannot free you from feeling jealous and heartbroken. A limited mind is impotent to cause any significant change, but it is prone to make mistakes. Love is the only answer."

It is interesting that my mind is not uneducated and believes in Love as the only true force in the universe. In your book- "An educated mind's strength lies in its unwavering confidence in the unmatched benevolent power of Love." And I am there, right here and now. Then what is blocking me from the realization of true Transformation? Are hidden issues buried deep in the subconscious?

"A belief in Love is not Love. Only when Love becomes an integral part of the mind, you will exercise its power. Just another mind's trick makes you think if you repeat: "I have unwavering confidence..." alas, you have it! It does not work this way. You may repeat it a million of times, "I have unwavering confidence in the unmatched benevolent power of Love," and nothing will change.

"There is always an exclusion, however. In some cases, depending on intensity, perseverance, and truly powerful confidence, this unwavering repetition may bring you into the world of Love. It happens rarely, and it did not happen to you because your ignorance is too deep. When you realize Love you do not need to repeat anything; you do not need even to say, Love. Do you repeat: "I am breathing"? You are just breathing without paying any attention to it. It is the same with Love when it realized, and you would wake up every morning grateful, happy, and fulfilled you will be lifted into a different world with no sorrow – the world of Love."

(It appears to me now, that transformed or enlightened individual will not depend on alcohol or nicotine. But then what about Nisargadatta, who was a chain smoker?). And another guy from Christian Science Church, very loved and respected, kind and bright, who was under the influence of alcohol on a daily basis.

"Masters may also be mistaken. You could read the chapter *Masters and Mistakes* in my upcoming book *Lester's wisdom III: Transformation.* Nisargadatta was an Indian teacher and like it is with nearly all Indian teachers his teaching is convoluted and rooted in the dogma of reincarnation. He was smocking because he did not have an inner peace of full realization. A fully realized person can never be a chain smoker or an alcoholic because when Love leads there is only beauty and enjoyment of life's every instant."

Maybe some individuals are not destined for real Transformation. My habitats - house and place in the city- are an expression of Love. Beautiful and harmonious. My everyday routine is to keep it that way. I love doing it. You say- "Anyone can realize Love." I did around me! And I do feel and experience compassion and understanding to people, which are not even my favorites.

"Your habitat is your squirrel cage with you endlessly spinning the same wheel of misery – a little satisfaction – and again back to misery… If your feeling of compassion was genuine, you would be compassionate towards yourself. With true Love, there is true compassion that will never make you feel miserable and heartbroken; it would never let you indulge in alcohol and smoking."

I admire this statement: "When Love is realized it celebrates the death of all negativity we had within. A (true) Love is not an emotion; it is expressed through its properties of understanding, acceptance, compassion, and kindness. When it comes to deeply negative situations, do not use the word love, instead, utilize Love's properties." I experience this in my life now. And it gives me great relief from the burden of being angry.

"We realize Love to be led by Love, to experience its peace and wisdom uninterruptedly, not just now and then…"

I am telling this to myself now every day. "Thanks for everything. I have no complaint whatsoever." Many times. It feels as the dark cloud is lifting off me.

"Well, this is a good practice, and it may lift you off your dreamland and to the world of Love because *gratitude* is the property of Love. However, until you purge the subconscious of negativity, you would have to constantly use a great deal of effort to overcome resistance and conditioning that would otherwise sabotage your every effort at becoming uninterruptedly *grateful*☺ I could see you are not able to use a *great deal of effort.*"

I know this and witnessing every day in me and around me: "It is not conscious mind but subconscious that makes people so different from one another. Subconscious is ruling the mind. "

Live each present moment completely and the future will take care of itself.
Fully enjoy the wonder and beauty of each instant.

"When you truly understand this you would engage *Transformation* without delay."

You said "Depending on the amount of the negative garbage hidden in one's past as well as the level of resistance and conditioning... some people may be less predisposed. It also may be a genome that carries negative inheritance. (That is for sure in my case!)

"The only difference between the one who is predisposed to Transformation and the one who is less predisposed is that the latter must let go of the laziness have to work more on educating the mind with *The Right Knowledge*, be more persistent, diligent and intense.

"You cannot know for sure if it is your case. If it is, realized Love would correct every imperfection."

As you can see from my testimony, my mind is totally and completely invested in Love, as Principle and ruling force. And I am practicing what I wholeheartedly believe in! But the negative garbage, hidden deep inside, still has great power in my life. I hide it well!

"Yes, your mind thinks about Love, but Love does not lead it. Your mind is talking all about Love with no results as all its blabber does not help you to change for the better. Thinking and talking is the mind's business that locks true Love out of your dreamland. You must see you do not know Love but know much about it. To know Love, to become Love you must realize it; all the talking in the word is of no help."

Live each present moment completely and the future will take care of itself.
Fully enjoy the wonder and beauty of each instant.

For some reason, it is easy for me to tell you all this. Your advice will be greatly appreciated. But, if there will be none, it is still good to know, that there is Yuri, who understands.
Love is All there is,

L.

Whether they are trifles or serious mistakes, most people keep blaming themselves for the rest of life. The ignorant mind creates this blaming habit. Let us look at the following situation from the Love's point of view. Love does not judge or criticize not only because of its benevolent nature. We cannot judge others or themselves also because on a deeper level most mistakes and attitudes are not people's fault. It is said, Jesus expressed this deeper understanding as *People do not know what they do,* which means that people are unaware most of the time. Even when they are aware, their level of awareness is low. When mind unaware, it makes mistakes.

Another, even more important reason is our cultural environment saturated with negativity. This reason is cause of all human suffering for it is erasing *The Right Knowledge* and the necessity of Love. When *The Right Knowledge* is absent what is left? Ignorance. Throughout this book, we are stressing the matter of loving upbringing. Could parents be blamed for not creating a loving environment for their children? Then, their grandparents also must be blamed for not creating a loving environment for their children and grandparents, and.... there is no end to blaming. Love knows *People do not know what they do*.

Love also knows that blaming does not change anything but only causes more negativity, more distress.

Peter came to Moscow from Germany looking for new business opportunities. Instead, he fell in love with 28-year-old Natasha. A year later Peter went back to Germany, and Natasha gave birth to a little girl Nastya. When Nastya was one month old, Peter invited Natasha and their little daughter to come to Munich.

When arrived at the Munich airport, Natasha was up for a shock. A little man came up to her, introduced himself as Peter's friend and said that Peter did not come because he has just got married.

That shock was never transformed into Love but kept influencing Natasha for the rest of her life. Now, at over 60, Natasha's conscious mind believes that shock is a long-forgotten, that she does not care about it any longer, that she never thinks about Peter and when she does, she is only grateful to Peter for gifting her with Nastya who grew up into a wonderful human being. If that were true, if that shock was released, Natasha would not be taking antidepressants for the rest of her life. Unfortunately, the subconscious forgets nothing.

When Peter passed away, Nastya casually mentioned, "There was some disturbance… Peter passed away… otherwise, everything is fine." Not only Natasha's subconscious kept remembering all this time that terrible shock. The negative shock was transferred from mother to the daughter. It helped to form Nastya's negative attitude towards her father. Seeing what Peter has done, such daughter's negative attitude towards father considered appropriate in dreamland. It is an example of the ignorance that unless transformed into Love, would keep causing life-long psychological harm. It will never happen in the world of Love.

A child-parent relationship is of a very sensitive nature. Even when the child does not remember one or both parents, he or she will think about them often throughout life. It is harmless. However, when parents did something wrong, that negativity will influence the child's life whether the child's conscious mind remembers it or not, for subconscious forgets nothing. The negativity, whether remembered or hidden in the subconscious can be eliminated only with *Transformation.*

"…But honestly, I can't say I love my parents 100%. There are some remains of rage, hate, and fear. My family's was a dramatic story, the story that is still alive in my mind after all these years. It is difficult to love people who destroyed almost everything they had for not being able to forgive each other. The hardest part is that of my mother who was daily killing herself from the age of 40 years on, with drinking, smoking 40 cigarettes a day, lying in bed watching TV and never caring for her health, her children or the house. I need to release all that. But please can you explain again to me why you said that releasing can't take you to the deeper subconscious and the methods you use to get there?"

Live each present moment completely and the future will take care of itself.
Fully enjoy the wonder and beauty of each instant.

This letter is an example of the powerful resistance program and conditioning that often are barring people from understanding this chapter. *Transformation* is a quite simple process. What makes it look complicated is Resistance and Conditioning – the mind's limitations that are justifying and guarding ignorance.

...Releasing cannot take you to the deeper subconscious for several reasons. Releasing remains in the realm of the limited mind while realized Love takes us beyond mind's limitations. Releasing is a man-created concept; thus, it cannot be without limitations while Love is our essence; it is free from limitations. In itself, releasing has no power while realized Love is the most powerful force in the human world. With every negative situation transformed into Love, we gradually begin to use this force. Our full possession of this force comes with the realization of Love.

- Learn how to watch you mind (explained below) so that you effortlessly know what is in there at every moment.

- Learn to love yourself unconditionally, regardless of the negativity you may presently harbor. You accumulated it you can eliminate/transform it. Giving yourself plenty of approval as often as possible is a wonderful way to start falling in love with yourself.

- Make irrevocable decision to transform your past into Love, regardless of what you presently feel about *Transformation*.

Live each present moment completely and the future will take care of itself. Fully enjoy the wonder and beauty of each instant.

- This chapter has everything you need to begin transforming your past into Love. You may find it useful to make some adjustments. Be creative.

- Read this chapter carefully until you feel comfortable with it.

- Resistance is usually expressed in laziness, procrastination, and unwillingness to do what needs to be done. It will trick you into asking questions. Asking questions is resistance way postponing what needs to be done. Do not fall into this trap. Try to get answers from within. Allow yourself to ask questions only after you failed to get them from within. Transform resistance into Love to your mind and move on with the process.

- It is our impatience and lack of trust in Love that blocks the answers from coming. If you did not get the answer from within, let the question in question stay in the back of yore mind. Be patient and utterly convinced the answer will surface. Be expectant like a pregnant woman is expectant of giving birth to a healthy baby.

- Do not philosophize, discuss, judge or criticize events and emotions you are transforming. Just witness it and transform.

Start practicing even if you have some unanswered questions. Trust yourself. In the process, most questions will lose their importance; others will be answered. Keep practicing, and like Lester, you may be able to enhance the process with your approach while using hints and suggestions given in this book.

Lester understood that he could transform into Love his attitude toward past negative events using logic, common sense and *something intuitive inexplicable else....* It is this *something inexplicable individual else* that the limited mind does not understand. Because of the lack of understanding the mind is trying to compromise *Transformation*. Here is how Lester describes this *something inexplicable individual else*:

Says Lester, "Conclusion: my happiness equates to my capacity to love.

"Then I devised a very deep process of trying to love others. I would review my past behavior. For instance, when I saw that I had been nice to a girl only because I wanted something from her, I would say, "You son-of-a-gun, Lester. Correct that!" Then I would love her for what she was, not what I wanted from her. I kept correcting myself until I could find nothing to correct."

It is what you need to create "a very deep process of trying to love others." That individualized approach may be your *unique inexplicable else*.

The limited mind creates problems and mistakes. It cannot help you to Happiness and Success because it cannot understand Love that is beyond its limitations. You need to accept this truth and keep working with your mind in its present condition. Alas, with your first successful *Transformation* you also will discover that which is contributing to *something inexplicable individual else*. It may or may not be expressed in words. It may be hints you get at doing something right. Most likely, it will be an intuitive discovery. Choose Love to be your guide at the start of the practice, and you will discover it sooner: you would sense it as encouragement, as an assurance of doing things right.

Do not get discouraged by initial failures. It took Lester some time to get results. We are in an incomparably better position than Lester was because we have a proven method while Lester was searching in the dark. You have the light of *The Right Knowledge*. Just do it! Transform into Love one particular situation. Stay with it, finish it then move to another event.

It may be even not a specific feeling of hate, anger or fear that you would be dealing with, it could be a welter of negativity that my friend (in the above example) convinced himself he had the right to feel. If he has thus convinced himself, he also can convince himself of the opposite.

Conditioning and Resistance, which are part of the ego or ignorance, are standing guard against Love because the realization of Love means death of the ego. An ego means judgment: *My family's was a dramatic story, the story that is still alive in my mind after all these years. It is difficult to love people who destroyed almost everything they had for not being able to forgive each other.* On the surface, it sounds right but only on the surface because we have neither right no need to judge, criticize or try to change someone's behavior. Love will never do that. The only ego believes it has right to barge into someone else's life whenever it wants.

When we say it from Love's point of view, the sentence will change because *Love's point of view* means the absence of the ego. When there is no ego, there is no judgment but compassionate witnessing. Not colored with emotions, a witness sees and speaks out the truth without being influenced by what is seen and said. When the above sentence is spoken from *Love's point of view,* it will reflect compassion, understanding, and acceptance: *Sadly, my parents destroyed their lives because they were not able to forgive each other.*

An ignorant mind may not want to give up negative emotions because there may be something masochistically "good" about keeping them in: a bittersweetness in experiencing their pain. Keep on going and transform this bittersweetness into Love.

The answer my friend is seeking maybe hidden in his letter, in this spontaneously written line: *"It is difficult to love people who destroyed almost everything they had for not being able to forgive each other."* Have you been able to forgive your parents and come to love them unconditionally? Forgiveness is compassion and understanding, which is Love.

You need to succeed only once, and the rest of the process will be easy, enjoyable.

People complain about their problems and difficulties but what do they do to alleviate them? Human ignorance too often is bordering on stupidity. True wisdom seems foolish to the ignorant mind. Because people do not believe in the power and magic of Love, because they have no Love, because they are lazy and do nothing to obtain *The Right*

Live each present moment completely and the future will take care of itself. Fully enjoy the wonder and beauty of each instant.

Knowledge, their cultural conditioning takes over and creates even more obstacles for them. Their Resistance program induces laziness. Consequently, the mind resists/rejects anything that is not in accordance with concepts adopted as truthful.

The mind's stronghold Resistance program can be compared with an impregnable wall. Unless rooted in Love our every experience and concept becomes a brick that reinforces this wall, cemented with ignorance. As we live, this wall of Resistance grows thicker and higher. The Resistance program is but our past; it is so powerful because it becomes an integral part of the subconscious. It is why most people are either ignoring Love and *Transformation* altogether or giving it up after just a few attempts. "Don't bother," the mind brags, "you're wasting your time," and a person quickly agrees: "Yeah, it is not for me, I have to find something else." There is no "something else" that is as powerful and effective as *Transformation*, except meditation, which would require more time.

Resistance is deeply embedded and cannot be released, destroyed, dissolved or otherwise eliminated. When we *transform* our negative past into Love, the Resistance program becomes obsolete because Love neither fights nor resists, it transcends our dreamland and elevates us into a higher realm of Love where there is no resistance but understanding, acceptance, and kindness.

In his book, *Thus Spake Zarathustra* Friedrich Nietzsche (who was purposefully misinterpreted by the Nazis and is misunderstood even today) speaks of the three human states of Camel, Lion, and Child. The Camel is lazy and dull; its Resistance program is all-powerful. The next higher state is Lion. When we realize we have been missing life while idling with crowds or in front of the idiot box, we begin to move up and out in our search for truth, and we roar. Our Resistance program is still strong, but it is weakening. With *Transformation,* we transcend resistance. When *Transformation* process is completed, the "wall" of resistance is left in dreamland, and a child emerges in the state of Love, an innocent, spontaneous, and loving child with adult experience.

Whatever state you are presently in, it will evolve, but only when you are determined to grow into a life of Happiness and Success. If you are already materially successful, your success is likely not fulfilling. The reason is your negative past, the "sorry scheme of things" you created unaware. Now being aware, re-mold your life into a life of your heart's desire.

Indeed, true Love is threatening the mind's supremacy. The limited mind is ignorant; it is also suspicious of Love because it cannot understand it. The mind's Resistance program is on and running, for until your past is transformed, the mind would not embrace Love. In its present state mind cannot know that it will enjoy its new position as the loving servant.

Until our past is *transformed*, the mind will continue to dominate and try to make decisions solely on its own. However, you can ask Love for advice on every matter.

*Live each present moment completely and the future will take care of itself.
Fully enjoy the wonder and beauty of each instant.*

Resistance can make it hard for you to accept someone you do not like but it cannot prevent you from asking Love for advice. Love's guidance will temporarily take you beyond resistance because Love knows neither resistance nor other limitations created by the mind. When you use it, it is inexhaustible. Decide for Love to be your guide and taste the power of Love.

The limited mind is very tricky, and it makes mistakes. Resistance is the mind's weapon, which it uses when something is threatening its supremacy. Nevertheless, all the mind's weapons are powerless against Love's guidance. Love's guidance will be of an incomparable help in your *Transformation* process.

Love is never mistaken. However, until Love is realized the mind is still in charge. It will make you doubt Love's advice and push for its solution. Until your past is transformed into Love, you may still follow your mind's advice. In the end, you will realize that Love's point of view is always the right point of view. When you want to make a decision, immediately, the mind comes up with suggestions. Listen to it, then relax, bring yourself into a more loving state and then ask for Love's advice on the same matter. You will be pleasantly surprised with what you get.

Appreciation and gratitude both are properties of Love. In every situation of your past and no matter how complex it was, find something or someone to be thankful and appreciative of. It also will help derail your Resistance program for a moment.

Live each present moment completely and the future will take care of itself.
Fully enjoy the wonder and beauty of each instant.

Gratitude… there is a wonderful Japanese story (adopted here from Zenkei Shibayama Roshi's *A Flower Does Not Talk*) which portrays this feeling:

A hundred and fifty years ago, there lived a woman named Sono whose purity of heart was respected far and wide. One day a fellow-Buddhist, having made a long trip to see her, asked, "What can I do to put my heart at rest?" She said, "Every morning and every evening, and whenever anything happens to you keep saying, "Thanks for everything. I have no complaint whatsoever." The man did as Sono instructed him for a whole year, but his heart still was not at peace. He returned to Sono crestfallen "I've said your prayer over and over and yet nothing in my life has changed; I am still the same selfish person as before. What should I do now?" Sono immediately said, "Thanks for everything. I have no complaint whatsoever." On hearing that the man was able to awake and return home with great joy.

This little story also demonstrates the power of the mind and the impotence of the religious prayer that was created to condition the mind into relying on the outside source. We are born self-sufficient. We are born with Love and its benevolent power. Rediscover Love, and you find everything you are looking for.

You may also employ the Sono suggestion of the gratitude mantra, yet this mantra would become truly effective when it is given and supervised by the enlighten Master as in the above example.

Still, some other helpful points are, *start small* and *enjoy every instant.* To help deal with resistance, start small and enjoy each instant of the process, regardless of having difficulties. For example, meditation is as much a threat to the mind's supremacy as *Transformation*, if not more. As soon as I learned of meditation, I decided to start meditating 15-minute sessions. Instantly, my Resistance program kicked in. The mind reminded me of the tasks to be accomplished at once, saying that I can meditate later. I was about to obey but realized that my mind simply had tricked me, for the tasks could surely wait for another 15 minutes.

I sat down determined not to move a muscle for at least 15 minutes and.... failed. Nevertheless, I was able to watch my mind uninterrupted for about twenty or thirty seconds. Learning from the experience, I made my next session only three minutes long. It took me several days to accomplish this small task. In less than six months of gradually increased sessions, I was able to meditate for one hour.

In the beginning, it may be better not to try to love someone you hate. Instead, go back to your early childhood memories and start with *transforming* into Love your earliest hurts. Let Love to guide you, use logic and common sense. Some negative memories are much stronger than the others are. Start with those that are easier to deal with and remind yourself to enjoy every moment of the process.

When you are transforming some negative event, there seems to be no place for enjoyment. However, you can still enjoy the process that leads you to Happiness and Success. These are two different things: the process and the event. Enjoy the process while working with the event. When any negativity, thought or emotion interferes with your enjoyment of the process, let it go or transform it into

*Live each present moment completely and the future will take care of itself.
Fully enjoy the wonder and beauty of each instant.*

Love. When you have transformed negativity of the event into Love, also enjoy the event that is now a loveable event regardless of what it has been in the past. The negative past (associated with it thoughts and emotions) cannot be released or let go of; it must be *transformed* into Love. On the other hand, negativity related to the process of *Transformation* can be released as it is resulting from your present-day activity.

My friend's girlfriend had a disastrous relationship with her former husband. It was all over about two years in the past, but she does not suspect how badly that experience is influencing her present relationship. "I don't think about him anymore," She said, "I have no feelings for him." With her permission, I explained to her the essence of *Transformation*. At once, I realized it was the wrong start. Tears ran from her eyes, and she exclaimed in utter disdain, "To love him!" She turned away, sobbing. Her subconscious kept "thinking" about him despite her trying to convince herself otherwise. Two years after that relationship ended, just a reminder of that man was too much for her. Nevertheless, later she became curious and started practicing *Transformation* but only a year later.

We can bury our hurts deep inside, so deep we do not even think about it any longer. However, it will keep working against us from the subconscious underground, silently sabotaging our relationships and goals.

I wrote about Jerry and Fritzie's 65-year-long relationship in *Freedom Technique: Path to Awareness and Love.* It was truly exceptional. Jerry and Fritzie are also a good example of the conditioning, which they inflicted upon themselves. Communism is a very appealing concept, but it is not executable because the masses' awareness is still low. Accepting this concept as doable, Jerry and Fritzie joined Canadian Communist Party at a very young age. In the sixties, they had learned about Soviet concentration camps and psychiatric prisons but did not give up their belief in the Soviet communism.

When 20 years later I asked them why they are so convinced of the concept that is proven time and time again to be wrong, Fritzie replied, "We are too old to change." Age is not an obstacle, but when we are knowingly harboring some negativity, we have to justify it at least to ourselves. It inevitably creates an inner conflict, which is quietly disturbing.

The mind may adopt concepts of communism and democracy as truthful, but Love accepts and understands what these concepts are. It is much more practical to adopt no concepts because any concept is just another limitation. With Love, we would accept all concepts but only for the people who created and adopted them. As to ourselves, we would not adopt any concept.

To reiterate, "I forgot about it a long time ago..." No, you did not; your subconscious forgets nothing. "Time heals" Wrong again. Only Love can heal your negative experiences. Every such excuse is just another trick of the mind caused by the resistance and conditioning – unfortunately, an often successful attempt to escape the truth.

In my meditation experience, the key was not only in starting small but also in learning how to enjoy every moment, regardless of failures. It was very hard to sit in a meditative posture. In the beginning, it was almost a torturous experience. Nevertheless, almost like a masochist, I made myself to enjoy the posture. It helped and within a few months, the posture seized to be a problem.

Teach yourself to enjoy each present moment completely. The mind will find many reasons why you cannot or do not need to enjoy each present moment, but the limited mind is also stupid. It knows not what is right but what it was taught to be right. The enjoyment helps in many ways, including an instant disabling Resistance program. It also makes your work more effective and pleasant. When you completed *Transformation*, you will be effortlessly enjoying every moment, but at the beginning of the process, you will often need to remind yourself of the enjoyment. Truly, why not to enjoy each moment of the *Transformation*? It is so natural to enjoy each instance of our growth, for when transformed into Love, every past situation moves us closer to the state of Love.

Moments of negativity are harmful. A moment of life not enjoyed is the moment lost. Life is short no matter how many years one lives. We must enjoy each instant; there should be no excuses. It will become obvious to you at some point during the *Transformation* process. In the course of practice, you will become more loving, more often and naturally guided by Love, and joy will happen naturally. You will also become a witness to the process. Though true witnessing is impartial, it is rooted in Love.

In 2002, there was a terrible fire in the Sequoias....

Live each present moment completely and the future will take care of itself. Fully enjoy the wonder and beauty of each instant.

The fire burned hole two feet deep in the trunk of the pine tree....

16 years past the tree stands as good and strong as ever. This is a true tenacity or an unconditional love of life.

Live each present moment completely and the future will take care of itself.
Fully enjoy the wonder and beauty of each instant.

This is what we should be in our practice of the *Transformation* – our journey to Love.

Conditioning

Is there any difference between pornography and violence when it splashed onto the screen of the movie theatre or Idiot box? Pornography and violence both are corrupting mind and cause psychological damage.

The Vikings were wild and ignorant people in desperate need of security. They believed they would get it by murdering everyone else. Recently, Hollywood created a TV series titled *Vikings*. Soon, the Russians created their own *Vikings* called Викинги, with even more blood on the screen.

Would the makers of this murderous piece of "art" ever create this horror if Love was their guide? It was said *people do not know what they do.* We all have Love – the Judge within – reminding us when we do something inappropriate. Thus, people know what they do. However, greed and fear – the two engines of ignorance – are hard to overcome.

Some people believe experiencing negative emotions is human. The right word, however, is stupid because negativity is detrimental to health and wellbeing.

You are mistaken thinking you are in control of your life. Is president of the US is in control of his life? It is a rhetoric question. Today, you may be happily married and have a business but… you or your wife may fall in love with someone else; your business may take a nosedive…. There seem to be no guarantees in life, which is true for everyone, poor and rich living in a dream world. Only when Love is realized, we come in control of our destiny.

It happens because the *Transformation* process wipes out our subconscious negativity, including *Conditioning* and *Resistance Program* – the barriers we have put in our way. Love is never mistaken. Intuition is the voice of Love. Following the Love's lead, its intuitive guidance, you would see clearly into the nature of dreamland and people.

Conditioning is a process used by individuals, societies, governments, religion, etc. to train, tame and otherwise habituate human mind with certain ideas, concepts, and ideology. There are numberless ways and methods used by various entities to condition human mind: government, corporate and religious propaganda; advertising; special interest groups' ideology and educational conditioning used in various learning institutions; social media, to name a few,

Conditioning means slavery. Realization of Love ends slavery.

For one who does not realize Love, it is impossible to withstand today's force of conditioning. When affected by this flood, which more than often is but misinformation, fake news, people get confused, disoriented. They cannot distinguish true journalism from fake news and fall victim to fear, uncertainty and insecurity.

When you enter words "fake news" in the search engine, it may identify fake news sites, yet, it is not only these sites, but the entire elite media is fake news. Speeches of the presidents and lawmakers are fake news; analyses and discussions broadcast by the media are mostly fake news.

When the mind is conditioned with negative concepts like Fascism, it becomes corrupted and self-distracted. It is the same with a concept of communism. When some ideology conditions the mind whether it is as good as democracy or as bad as fascism, it becomes utterly resistant to any other ideological concept; it does not want to hear about Love. Religious conditioning is one of the worst as it is dividing peoples and nations and destroying unity.

Why practice something so deeply ignorant, something that helped to destroy millions of lives, that was created to enslave and control? Instead, explore Dao and Zen that liberate. Religion is nearly dead in Europe, and the number of believers in the US is rapidly declining. Some statistics show 90% of Americans consider themselves Christians. In reality, this number is less than 30%. The other 60% are not the true believers, as they admit they call themselves Christians only because they have been brought up this way. Thus, people's awareness is on the rise.

The military that aims to turn a human being into a heartless robot is a graphic demonstration of the most harmful conditioning. Consequences of the conditioning by the military are tragic as it creates brutal, psychologically unstable humans.

A mind conditioned is the mind controlled. This control is effectively exercised from without. We cannot control the mind with conditioning. Only with Love, we can exercise natural, effortless and beneficial mind control.

I love this quote as it also is suggesting how one can effectively avoid conditioning:

Believe not because some old manuscripts are produced, believe not because it is your national belief, believe not because you have been made to believe from your childhood, but reason truth out, and after you have analyzed it, then if you find it will do good to one and all, believe it, live up to it and help others live up to it.

Whatever concept you are about to accept, drop it unless it conforms to this quote, for Buddha speaks here of true Love. Adopt only concepts that measure up to Love. However, there are no such concepts☺ because every concept whether negative or positive will not measure up to Love but limit it. Any concept can be understood and accepted but only for the sake of the people behind it, but it must not be adopted. When not adopted, a concept will not influence you. It will become a piece of information that you may either use or discard. Adopting means accepting a concept as being true in the world of Love, which will log it into the subconscious and create another limitation.

Every concept is contributing to conditioning. Love is intuitive and is beyond all concepts and conditioning. If you are employing a mantra or an affirmation, unless it is rooted in Love, it is not for your benefit. When an affirmation is rooted in Love, it will measure up to the above quote. You may check any of your concepts against this quote and learn that all of them could be discarded for only Love *is* most effective at *doing good to one and all*.

Conditioning and resistance are reinforcing each other. Depending on the kind of the conditioning, as soon as it adopted and became a part of ourselves, it can also be deadly.

Our society is conditioning people with the belief that democracy is real in this country. Nonetheless, a true democracy cannot coexist with inequality. When there is an inequality, our democracy is true only for the rich.

What Buddha saying is but a tribute to Love as well as it is a warning of the conditioning. Are you an individuality or a personality, which is individuality, conditioned by the philosophies, religion, teachings, and concepts – a lost individuality? Transform all acquired dross into Love and discover your open and loving individuality anew.

Stay away from crowds.

Last year I published an unusual and beautiful love story *The 41st*. This true story demonstrates with unparalleled vividness a deadly impact of the ideological/cultural conditioning. At all time, one's awareness is in a direct proportion with the degree of the conditioning. The more your subconscious and the conscious mind is conditioned/clogged with information related to life, whether negative or positive, the less you are aware.

When conditioning is predominantly negative awareness falls to its lowest, as in the case of the Fascist Germany, USSR or Mao's China where countless millions were killed by their compatriots conditioned with the murderous ideology.

In personal relationships, in the beginning, conditioning that has been deeply embedded into the subconscious may be temporarily overridden by the excitement of a new relationship. The subconscious never "forgets" its conditioning and will strike a blow to its owner at a time least expected.

A man refused using conventional treatment and for over six years is fighting prostate cancer with cannabis oil and Ozone therapy. At the same time, his Idiot box is on displaying deadly violent trash.

I asked him to consider the damage this "art" is causing by slowing down his healing efforts, especially when the subconscious is the most receptive and vulnerable – when he is falling asleep with the violence exploding on the screen. He got angry: "I know what I am doing! It is my only escape from pain!"

When he came to the US, he surrounded himself with TV screens to learn English, so the story goes. Now, forty years later this conditioning has become deeply engraved into his subconscious. "I know violence is not good," he said later, "but I am in control of my feelings."

Of course, this is nonsense, because he is not even able to control his outbursts of anger and irritation when something goes wrong in his household. Everyone around him is suffering during these fits of anger; he also is suffering from guilt and inability to control himself.

The Realization of Love eliminates both conditioning and resistance. If you are selfish, you may try to condition yourself into being kind with affirmations, logic and common sense. You may also use releasing. However, something will happen, and your kindness will go down the drain. You can achieve a permanent state of kindness only with *Transformation* or Classic meditation and nothing else what so ever.

It is the same with business relationships and decisions: when there is no Love, our subconscious is in charge and is silently influencing everything we do.

The subconscious is ruling the mind. However, when Love is realized, Love becomes our only ruler. Unlike the mind influenced by the subconscious, Love is influenced by nothing and is mistake-proofed.

Witnessing the mind

Witnessing the mind and loving yourself is of the paramount importance as it is the fundamental practice on the path. It is also highly beneficial in everyday life. Witnessing the mind can be done only in the present. When witnessing becomes your natural state and you would effortlessly watch the mind (a silent, an intuitive part of the mind watching emotional thinking process (ETP), you would find yourself living in the present.

To live each present moment completely and fully enjoy the wonder and beauty of each instant could be experienced only in the present. Thus, mustering witnessing the mind, you will also realize a great secret of life: letting the future to take care of itself.

No progress could be made on the path without mastering witnessing the mind and unconditionally loving yourself.

There is a difference between witnessing and watching the mind. In the beginning, you are watching your mind, which process also could involve some emotions. As you progress, watching turns into an unperturbable (emotionless) witnessing and you become fit to the following description of great Hui Neng:

In your contact with all types of men,
Ignore faults of others.
Be indifferent to their merit or demerit, good or evil.
For such an attitude accords with the imperturbability of the essence of Mind.

Here *be indifferent* means to have no thoughts and emotions related to the "watching" the others. As you know, there is no such thing as indifference as term *indifference* is serving to cover hidden negativity. How amazingly timely things happen when we let it happen, when we let *the future to take care of itself.* We let it happen when we are loving and peaceful. It naturally happens when Love leads us. Everyone I met in life can be categorized as a loving or not a loving person. Without exception, loving people have fewer problems. They are more content, accepting and patient. People, who were denied Love in their childhood and had no opportunity to rediscover it in their adult life, usually are irritable, impatient, often getting angry, knowing no contentment.

The resistance of the *Transformation* is the resistance of Love. The mind has been our guide for such a long time; it made us subjects to itself. The mind does not want to give up control for it trusts nothing but itself. The mind resists choosing Love's guidance because of our thinking habit: we love to think, but also hate it when mind keeps thinking on its own and we cannot control it. Love, on the other hand, does not think but communicate its message via intuition, which is another wonder to the limited mind.

In most people, Love was blocked in childhood by the unhappy environment. When parents and schoolteachers lack *The Right Knowledge*, negativity is inflicted under the pretense of being necessary for survival. The resistance program, created in early childhood, becomes the safeguard of the negative conditioning. It will do its best to make sure you reject witnessing and living in the present. It will keep telling you would never be able to let future take care of itself because you must work hard to secure a good future.

When Love is realized, we naturally, effortlessly let the future take care of itself. To the dreamland dweller, however, the idea of the future taking care of itself seems ridicules because the limited mind being itself a ridicules tool of pushing and striving cannot understand how it can be done.

Nevertheless, occasionally, it has happened to each of us. It is called *The Lost Keys Phenomenon.* When some keys are misplaced, the best thing to do is to let go of the search, knowing that the keys will surface. It always does.

The lost keys phenomenon can be applied to any goal, as well as... to *the future taking care of itself;* only without an intuitive calm of the realized Love, we are not aware of it. In the process of the *Transformation,* the mind's limitations are being dissolved, and the mind begins eagerly participate in the process. When Love is realized, *the future takes care of itself* because now an educated mind is led by Love, and is listening to the Love's intuitive guidance. Love is unmistaken; it "knows" what we need and how to deliver it (which is another puzzle to the limited mind). Because the mind is no longer dominating, it becomes an interpreter of Love's intuitive messages. In reality, the mind is not interpreting intuitive information but is dressing it in words.

A drop of the sea carries within all the sea. Each present moment carries within all life, including your life. It is forever old because it holds our entire past. It is forever new as it has our every new experience. When the negative subconscious past is purified, *we live each present moment completely, let the future take care of itself* and experience the wholeness of Life.

The society teaches pushing and striving, which is the only thing left to do in the absence of Love. There is a big difference between using force and applying strength.

When Love is realized, the society is left behind together with its forces and is no longer able to influence us. A force is of the ego while strength is of Love. *Mastering others requires force*, says the Tao, *Mastering the self, needs strength*.

Most people understand that Love is important, but they are not guided by Love because the mind accepts Love only on the surface and on its terms, which is "I love this person, but I hate the other one." Because Love is beyond the mind's conditioning, the mind cannot understand (true) Love's absolute importance for a life of Happiness. When you educate the mind with *The Right Knowledge*, it will understand and begin to co-operate with *Transformation*. Still, even when co-operating, the mind will often try to subvert *Transformation*. Educate your mind with *The Right Knowledge,* and teach it how to watch itself.

Just watch the mind without reacting to your thoughts, as if you are *watching* someone else's mind or as you are watching a train pass by. There is nothing complicated about it. Consistently remind yourself of the *watching*. Soon you will notice how gaps of quiet in between your thoughts dramatically increase. Watch the mind until *watching* becomes as effortless as breathing. By this time, you will know your mind well.

With practice, the mind will begin to watch itself without any effort on your part. At that time, you will be able effortlessly and instantly to let go/transform into Love any negative thought and emotion. That is how simple it is: decision and watching, watching, and watching, that is all.

Live each present moment completely and the future will take care of itself.
Fully enjoy the wonder and beauty of each instant.

Learning how to watch the mind may be likened to learning how to ride a bicycle. Until we begin to practice, it seems very difficult to ride on two wheels. Once we learned how to ride, it becomes natural; we do not ever think about it again. It is the same with witnessing the mind. First, it seems a strange and difficult thing to do. However, as you begin practicing the ease and benefits of the witnessing become manifest.

Always remain in the present. No matter what is happening in your inner and outer world stay in the present moment. Do not follow your mind's movement to the past or future. Just watch it. There is a big difference between daydreaming and witnessing the mind now.

For example, *nostalgia* is negative because it makes you idle in the past. It is also adding a sort of "sweet sadness" to the experience and making you regret or enjoy some things you did. When you would consciously witness *nostalgia,* it will show what needs to be transformed into Love.

When witnessing the mind, you could see where it is taking you. You begin to understand that you did not get too far because you were driving your car of life with both accelerator and brakes on. You finally recognize the culprit: your past – the accumulated negativity hidden in the subconscious. You recognize its tremendous influence.

The mind is naturally empty and only when it remains empty, without grasping and rejecting, can it respond to natural things without prejudice. It should be like a river gorge with swan flying overhead. The river has no desire to retain the swan; yet, the swan's passing is traced by its shadow without any omission. Another example: a mirror

Live each present moment completely and the future will take care of itself. Fully enjoy the wonder and beauty of each instant.

will reflect things perfectly, whether they are beautiful or ugly. It never refuses to show a thing; nor does it retain the thing after it is gone. The mind should be as open as this.

Ling-Ching-Hsi

The mind opens naturally with the realization of Love.

Yuri,

I had one come up from 5th grade, many years ago, I was in a class of about 30 boys, and one of the boys was having a birthday party for the next weekend.

I watched him as he handed out invitations; one by one they were passed out until he had run out. Three others and I were NOT INVITED to the party.

At the time I was devastated... And all that came back up and I felt so hurt, and I could feel my stomach and everything tighten up.... I then transformed it and sent love to the other boy and forgave him and sent love to all my classmates and me. As I did this, my emotions exploded, and I cried it out! It took about 15-20 minutes, and it was so intense.

After it was done, I felt like I dropped a ton of weight...the results were amazing, it was about three days ago, and I never had results like this. I feel so much lighter!

Just this event that was 15 minutes of my life so many years ago...it seems impossible. The leverage it had over me was overpowering. This one Transformation has already made a huge difference in my life. I am amazed!

Live each present moment completely and the future will take care of itself.
Fully enjoy the wonder and beauty of each instant.

This is what Lester meant, no doubt.

Depending on the amount of the negative garbage hidden in one's past as well as the level of resistance and conditioning, some people are predisposed to *Transformation* and realization of Love others are less predisposed. It also may be genome that carries negative inheritance.

The only difference between the one who is predisposed to Transformation and the one who is less predisposed is that the latter would have to let go of being lazy and work more on educating the mind with the *Right Knowledge*, be more persistent, diligent and intense.

Who in his right mind would reject Love? Excuses such as "It is not for me" are created by the Conditioning and Resistance, which is ignorance. For only an ignorant mind rejects Love.

Become your own best teacher

> Oh, come with old Khayyam, and leave the wise
> To talk; one thing is certain that life flies;
> One thing is certain, and the rest is lies...
> The flower that once has blown forever dies.

What is life's purpose if not a true Happiness? Our life has no meaning unless we find Happiness and share it by helping the others to find it. When it happens, we fulfill our purpose. We also would help to the world's oneness against the negative trends of war, fraudulent government, violent entertainment, pornography, and many other disasters plugging humanity.

When you make an irrevocable decision for a life of Happiness to be your purpose, also decide to become your teacher. Do not become a victim of the self-proclaimed gurus and teachers, their seminars and books. Do not get enticed by the spiritual industry's promises. Leave search and start practicing. Most people on the path spend too much time searching, attending seminars, and studying teachings. It is the unnatural learning process. When you meditate, it takes much time for a good reason. When you are spending endless years reading teachings and attending seminars, it is waste of life for no one ever found Love and freedom in the crowd.

There are numberless spiritual teachings. For some reason, we may be drawn to one or another. However, to everything there is a season and the time for every purpose under heaven, says the Preacher. You have done many searches, and you do not want to spend your life doing it over and over again.

You know true answers come from within. It will happen sooner when you become your teacher.

You have no choice because you already are your own best teacher with all the knowledge available to you. The question is how to access it, and the answer is Love. Love is all you need to access the necessary information. Love is but a secret valve that opens the flow of intuition carrying information you need at any given moment. Only with Love, you would find all you need.

Live each present moment completely and the future will take care of itself.
Fully enjoy the wonder and beauty of each instant.

For millenniums, the wise were saying that a human being is his own best teacher. It is even more so today with much information freely available. Lester said much about Love, Happiness, and Freedom. Andrew Carnegie provided an enlightening example of Love's infinite power in business.

We have a proven method of *Transformation*. We have Carnegie's example where Love helped to create the greatest business success of all time, where Rockefellers and J, P. Morgans fell flat on their face with anger greed. We also have a present-day example of *The Giving People* and numerous examples of the people led by Love. We have everything necessary to become our own best teachers.

Soon, you realize your life started to change for the better. To say it more accurate, now you are steering your life in the direction you have envisioned. *The Transformation*, which awakens an intuitive guide of Love, helps to develop awareness, to rout events of your life in the necessary direction, to make your health sound, and to harmonize your life with the pulse of the universe.

Is there any other state of being which is greater than Love bordering with peace of Freedom? With Love, you recognize your talent, employ it and achieve Success. With Love, you find Happiness. You remember that incredible feeling of falling in love. You would experience the same feeling of joy with a touch of silliness at the end of the *Transformation process*. Only now, this feeling, this state of knowing and loving mind will be forever.

As you complete transforming your past, you will find yourself at the "border." Beyond this border is Freedom. At that moment, you may be subtly persuaded to move on, which is a definite sign of your ability to find Freedom. Following is a quote from *The Count of Monte Cristo*.

"God can change the future. He cannot alter even an instant of the past."

God cannot change either past or future; the only loving mind can. The calm power derived from a daily practice can transform what seems to be a disaster into a blessing.

Live each present moment completely and the future will take care of itself.
Fully enjoy the wonder and beauty of each instant.

Exhibition of handmade art at Lake Quaroun, Egypt, 2016

Talent

In 1976, I was filming on St. Croix, Virgin Islands. On Friday evening, hungry and tired after twelve-hour shooting day, we stopped at a small cafe set on top of the cliff high above the sea. The whole structure seems to be floating as the only transparent sheets of light plastic curtains separated a cozy mahogany cafe interior from the darkening blue Caribbean leisurely reflecting crimson of the setting sun.

Suddenly, there was a sound, a song, and the feelings it evoked were incredible. I think I have never felt anything like that before... nostalgia, a little sadness with a little warmth were intertwining with love and joy, and some great unknown energy, altogether inexplicably pleasant and serene. The song was *Hotel California*. It has just begun its triumphant conquest of the world.

Recently I stumbled upon the blog and got curious with hundreds of fans arguing over the song's meaning.

Is it possible to define the meaning of the Sunset reflecting memories of the dying day in the forever rising and falling waves of the ocean?

In 2008, Don Felder described the origins of the lyrics: "Don Henley and Glenn wrote most of the words. All of us kind of drove into LA. at night. Nobody was from California, and if you drive into LA at night.... you can just see this glow on the horizon of lights, and the images that start running through your head of Hollywood and all the dreams that you have, and so it was kind of about that...."

"... kind of about that." Even a song's writer cannot define its meaning because.... there is no meaning. At the same time, everyone who is listening to the song creates his or her meaning. There are as many meanings as there are listeners, which mean... no meaning that can be defined. Then what is there if there is no meaning? Hints, beats of memories and feelings, reflections and associations that are not clearly defined, which all together creates a very special mood, a very individual mood to each of us, corresponding with our vision and imagination....

That's *Talent*! And there are no definitions. The song is a stroke of genius. No one can describe this stroke, except…. critics. A song critic is often a failed songwriter. It is the same with success coaches who are teaching success based on achievements of fortune creators. A fortune builder creates with his *Talent* a unique song called Fortune and no one can explain how he did it, even the creator himself. This is why many of *The Giving People* use words like "luck," "genes" and "being born to loving parents."

How foolish we are not to recognize what we are best fitted for and can perform, not only with ease but with pleasure, as masters of the craft. More than one able man I have known had persisted in blundering in an office when he had a great talent for the mill and had worn himself out, oppressed with cares and anxieties, his life a continual round of misery, and the result of the last failure. I never regretted parting with any man so much as Mr. Kloman. His was a good heart, a great mechanical brain, and had he been left to himself. I believe he would have been glad to remain with us. Offers of capital from others--offers which failed when needed--turned his head, and the great mechanic soon proved the poor man of affairs.

Andrew Carnegie in *Autobiography*

How foolish we are not to recognize what we are best fitted for and can perform, not only with ease but with pleasure, as masters of the craft.

There are many mysteries in life that so far no one can solve. From life itself being a mystery to our solar system

Live each present moment completely and the future will take care of itself. Fully enjoy the wonder and beauty of each instant.

and the universe being great mysteries. There is also something called *Talent,* which so far is an unsolved mystery that happens to be a prime reason for success in any field of life. It's important to remember that the word success (small's') identifies any success, small or large in any field when it is achieved without Love, whereas Success (capital 'S') identifies accomplishment of any size made in any field of life when Love guides us.

In the chapter *True Dreamers of the American Dream: The Giving People,* you'll find some of them are using word "luck" as being one of the reasons for their success. What is luck? To some it means being born in America, the land of opportunities; others believe luck means lucky genes or being born to loving parents. However, luck has nothing to do with success and Success.

In the Tao, every day something is "dropped" so it does not influence upon us... When we are in search of truth, ideally, all acquired knowledge pertinent to the human world needs to be set aside because most of it is not genuine or right. If acquired knowledge about your life was genuine, you would be now led by Love and live a life of Happiness. It is impossible to evade influence of the acquired knowledge with a wishful thinking, positive thinking, and mantras or by any other means. Exceptions here are extremely rare.

Mantras have no power that is often ascribed to them. The power may be generated only by you. The mantra is an aid to meditation. We may start meditation session with a mantra in order initially to calm the mind. As mind gets calmer, it also gets easier to watch. Mantra cannot eliminate or neutralize forces; it cannot break obstacles, the only awakened mind can. When calm and loving, the mind would break any obstacle and neutralize any force. For a mantra to become a useful aid to meditation and *Transformation,* it must be rooted in Love. You must believe unconditionally in the meaning you ascribe to the mantra.

Nevertheless, the best practice is to drop all aids and witness the mind.

Classic meditation (see: *Classic Meditation* in the Addendum, below) or *Transformation* will eliminate negativity as well as "disarm" an acquired knowledge that will not be erased but will lose its ability to influence. When this happens, we would be able to use any information and be not affected by it, as Love will be our only guide.

Right knowledge leads to *Transformation* and Classic meditation. It may be a hint, teaching or a quote that will result in a sudden revelation.

Believe not because some old manuscripts are produced. Believe not because it is your national belief. Believe not because you have been made to believe from your childhood, but reason truth out, and after you have analyzed it, then if you find it will do good to one and all, believe it, live up to it and help others live up to it.

Attributed to Buddha

Live each present moment completely and the future will take care of itself.
Fully enjoy the wonder and beauty of each instant.

It is not important whether there was a Buddha. It makes no difference who said these beautiful words. It is important to understand the meaning of the saying. The wisdom of the Universe is expressed in it. When consciously employing this saying you instantly lift yourself beyond conditioning and resistance that you presently have in great measure. Employ it always, and you will realize that no matter how good is our culture, society, and country, it is yet too far from being a paradise. Though the Paradise is right here – within, you waste life fighting and striving while trying to find it without. Disappointment and frustration follow, and a rollercoaster keeps tumbling up and down, up and down, up and down.... and there seems to be no end to this distress.

The calm power derived from a daily practice can transform what seems to be a disaster into a blessing. With *The Right Knowledge*, you will see things through and through. Among other things, you would perceive that in relation to success, the word luck is meaningless, as it does not define the reason behind success; it may also be misleading implying that anyone can get lucky at creating, for example, great wealth.

People are often getting confused with definitions such as luck, success, and *Talent*. A common understanding of big financial success, almost any success is usually attributed to luck. However, everyone who rose from rags to riches has created wealth because they possessed a *Talent* of creating wealth. The reason for this confusion is the *Talent's* mystery that is impossible to define. Another reason is the success industry's total absence of *The Right Knowledge.*

A substance creates a major difference between definitions of luck and *Talent.* Luck has no substance. It is an empty word, which is used to compensate for lack of knowledge of the cause. On the other hand, *Talent* has great substance to it. The most important part of this "substance" is still a mystery, which makes *Talent* a mystery that causes people to confuse it with "luck."

Only as a distant approximation may we allude to *Talent* as being a set of special qualities, where each quality must be uniquely individual and harmonious with all other qualities to create success in any field of life. The more fine-tuned and harmonious the alliance of these qualities, the greater is success or Success. When most of these qualities are lacking, there is no *Talent,* and there can be no success made in that field. Nevertheless, anyone can discover his/her *Talent* and succeed in a field that is harmonious with that *Talent.*

Every *Talent* is purely individual. Every original (ass opposed to inherited) great wealth has was with a unique individual *Talent,* even like song *Hotel California* was created with a unique *Talent* or *Gone with the Wind,* and *The Razor's Edge* was written by the people of great *Talent. Talent* cannot be acquired like skill, for *Talent* is inborn and indefinable. However, anyone can discover his or her *Talent* with Love.

Andrew Carnegie, John D. Rockefeller, Henry Ford, J. P. Morgan and every other person who rose from rags to riches were born with a *Talent*. There is a degree of *Talent* as well as a quality to *Talent*. A degree of the *Talent* characterizes the size of a corresponding success, whereas quality in the *Talent* means presence or absence of Love.

Do you know of any popular song that is about violence, or pornography? There is none. With a few rare exceptions of the psychologically depraved persons, including everyone who is involved in the production of the pornography and violence in the entertainment industry, people detest violence and pornography. With only a few exceptions, the songs are all about love and relationship between a man and a woman.

When a song is created, and it becomes popular, this creation must have been rooted in Love; there also must be the *Talent*. People love and enjoy songs about love, they love and enjoy the subject of love more than any other subject, then why not to make movies featuring beautiful love stories that demonstrate the power of Love?

There are several reasons why despite people's loving the subject of love more than they love any other subject, the majority of films are featuring violence. The main reason is the demand: the little aware masses get excited about violence. It will certainly change with time, with a higher level of awareness. Another reason is that some filmmakers either have no *Talent* or there is a *Talent,* but it lacks the quality of Love thus turning a filmmaker into a robot driven by the subconscious negativity, mostly greed.

In the absence of Love, the mind endowed with a *Talent* can become a very tricky mind. It may convince itself it can get away with murder.... and it does, for we become what we believe. However, if a person is still sane, it will not commit the actual murder. Instead, they will express their conviction in writing a violent novel (The Godfather) or creating a violent motion picture (Chain Saw Massacre), etc. If a talented mind lost sanity, it could create a murderous philosophy, like Hitler and Stalin.

When a *Talent* is lacking the quality of Love, it cannot create a gifted love story. Instead, it would travel an easy way of least resistance and capitalize on people's lower nature using violence as a bait. However, like any other human being, a talented filmmaker may sometimes have a glimpse of Love. When this spark of Love happens, even when Love is not realized, *ET* is made, or a striking love story is created. The ignorance would praise *The Godfather* with the same enthusiasm as *ET,* and spread violence throughout the world.

Media promotes successful, talented people. You follow them on the social networks, but do you know who you are following. As it is with every other hype created by the media and production companies, we do not see the truth hiding behind the hype. The truth is many celebrities are ignorant people devoid of Love. In my experience, a wonderful actor Robin Williams also happened to be dishonest, as he has stolen several original ideas from the screenplay we submitted for his consideration.

Kim Kardashian's worth is $175 million. She is boasting on the Internet about helping others. She does not share her wealth. A little bit here and a little there, that's all. However, she sells used clothing on E-bay at a high price and gives away from the proceeds 20% -- a minimum required by the E-bay.

Steven Spielberg who is worth $2.5 billion refused to join 137 billionaires who pledged 50% to 100% of their wealth to charities. He shies away from the less fortunate but spends $400 million on his luxuries yacht.

During my Internet session, someone said that Spielberg earned his money lawfully and is entitled to do with it whatever he wishes. It is true; Spielberg did not rob a bank. However, the rich have created finance laws. These laws are devoid of Love and a provision of sharing the wealth. There is also a moral aspect to it, which is inevitably considered by those who are led by Love.

George Clooney is a wonderful actor. He is also a talker, jumping eagerly on every cause. However, when it comes to sharing, he prefers to purchase $36 million villa in Italy to entertain himself and his guests. How much is he giving? Do not waste time trying to find it out.

Regretfully, there are many more examples of ignorance in the entertainment industry. The people cannot be blamed, however, because they have been brought up this way, nurtured by their parents, school, and society. Nevertheless, why to follow ignorance? If you wish to follow, choose someone like Judith Falkner, a billionaire and a wonderful person who pledged 99% of the fortune to help the needy. The best thing to do is not to waste time on the following, but to follow your own growth.

A similar situation exists in human life as every human either has or lacks the quality of Love. Nevertheless, we all possess the *Talent* to realize Love. It is usually hidden under a pile of rubble and needs to be re-discovered. Suffering, problems, disappointments, and glimpses of satisfaction will forever keep turning one after another until the realization of Love will disassemble this rollercoaster.

Mozart was writing symphonies since he was five years old, which makes it obvious that *Talent* cannot be learned, thus, it cannot be emulated. No matter how hard one would try, without having the same *Talent,* he will not be able to reach the supremacy of Mozart. Is it ever possible to have the same as someone else's *Talent*?

When I came to Los Angeles, my agent convinced me to audition for a part in an independent movie. I did OK, but far from being great. Then the producer invited me to his office and asked if I want to act. I pulled myself together and said I wanted to try, but now I see I have no talent. Why, he said, you did quite well? I had to explain that I felt miserable and ashamed because I saw that I was not good enough, that acting should be a joyful performance with little or no effort, that I don't want to be just another mediocrity. He laughed, and we had a good chat about the Red Empire.

The eBay Chairman Pierre Omidyar launched *First Look Media* in late 2013 with the aim of presenting new forms of independent journalism. Would Pierre be able to create a great wealth of over $7 billion without having a *Talent*?

What made Pierre pledge a major share of his assets to charitable causes if not Love?

What can be done when because of some unfortunate circumstances we are not able to utilize our *Talent*? When Love is realized, even if we cannot employ our *Talent*, Love will guide us to the most beneficial scenario, whether it is schooling, employment or a partnership, and enable us to create a life of Happiness.

Live each present moment completely and the future will take care of itself. Fully enjoy the wonder and beauty of each instant.

Saturn Mountains

Think Imagination

All that you are is the result of what you have thought and imagined.

"*Imagination* is everything. It is a preview of life's coming attractions." Albert Einstein

We have an imagination because our life is shaped by the four elements: Environment, Emotional-Thinking-Process (ETP), *Imagination*, and the subconscious influence. There would be no progress without *Imagination*. No *Imagination* means a dull unfulfilled life. A journey to the

95

life of Happiness and Success starts when you imagine having a life of Happiness and Success.

When we do not use *Imagination*, it is still at work. However, uncontrolled, it would contribute to chaos in individual life and a life of humanity. We literary imagine/create our life and then move in to experience our creation. When we are established in *imagining*/creating with Love, we experience Happiness and Success.

We think mostly in pictures. If I ask you not to think a monkey, your mind still would be picturing a monkey. It happens not because our mind does not recognize the word "not," as some people think. It happens because an average mind is infected with negativity protected by the Resistance program and mental Conditioning cannot be controlled. Instead, the mind's limitations are in control. A powerful *Imagination* is a gift, yet, uncontrolled it creates problems.

Donald Trump is a unique example of the powerful *Imagination*. Just think of it: with a few million dollars, he created a seven billion-dolor empire. He created his reality show. He decided and alas! He is the US President. Like in the lives of Carnegie, Rockefeller, JP Morgan, and millions upon millions of successful Americans, *Imagination* plays a fundamental role in every success. However, *Imagination* alone will not bring true Success and Happiness; there must be Love.

Donald Trump also is a wonderful example of outright ignorance. It proves once again that the others may view a deeply ignorant person as a very successful one (John

Kennedy, Ronald Regan, Barack Obama, to name a few true losers in Happiness) where the meaning of success, created by the success industry is a degenerate meaning of the true Success. As it is with majority of the rich, Trump's success dose not bring Happiness. Trump is getting angry, annoyed and irritated. In business, he proved to be an arrogant and greedy person, unwilling to share his success. Thus, Donald Trump happens to be an unhappy spiritual bankrupt and an ordinary fraud.

Several times Andrew Carnegie mentioned *imagination* in his *Autobiography* and other books, each time stressing its importance for success. Everyone has this gift; only most people know neither of the paramount importance it plays in shaping a life nor how to use it. Like any other quality, *imagination* can be developed to a very high degree. The *Transformation* and realization of Love enable uppermost *Imagination*.

In a dream, we often have incredible experiences. We may travel to distant lands fling without any mechanical means. In a dream, we may span many years of time. A dream is a dream, but there is something special about it. It tells as of our mind's ability to *imagine* amazing things and experience them as reality.

Imagination is a complex, multifaceted phenomenon, but it is easy to develop and use knowingly. Are those dream things that amazing? Jules Vern imagined and described a submarine many decades before it was thought about. Was his *imagination* able to tap into the future? Somerset Maugham effectively used this creative ability. While falling asleep, he would command his mind to create a new story. Upon awakening, the story would be ready in his mind.

Often, the border between real and unreal is blurred. Still, with *imagination,* the mind is easily crossing the borders. *Imagination* is freely creating anything in both worlds, even things seemingly unbelievable. In the world of dreams, when it is unobstructed, it is much easier for the *imagination* to create.

The greater is your power of *imagination* the easier it is to accomplish a goal.

Every misfortune brings with it the seed of even greater advantage. Aid this knowledge with *imagination,* keeping in the back of your mind an outcome you want to experience. In mind, your goal is already accomplished. Now you are expecting it to materialize. Love and *Imagination,* as well as the absence of the negativity about the goal, will lead to Success. However, when the subconscious is not cleansed of the negative past, this hidden negativity would continue to influence and often subvert your decisions. Why is Trump so successful? Because he is convinced, he is invincibly successful. However, with all that success Trump, like everyone else is riding an infamous rollercoaster where there is not even a vestige of the (true) Happiness, only glimpses of satisfaction alternating with much misery.

I heard it many times people saying, "A million of dollars will make me happy." It will make life easier, but there will be no Happiness unless your subconscious negative past is transformed into Love for only Love brings Happiness when it is realized.

Throughout his busy years, Carnegie kept in mind thought of gratitude to the man who introduced him to *The Right Knowledge* when Andrew was fourteen years old. He was convinced he also would help young people to receive *the precious treasures of knowledge and imagination through which youth may ascend.* It is these initial thoughts aided by the powerful *imagination* resulted in Carnegie's creation of over 3000 free libraries in the United States, England and his native Scotland, followed by giving back to people his entire fortune of $320 billion (adjusted for inflation).

Since high school, I was convinced I could write. I was writing diaries, then – scripts for my documentary films, then feature film screenplays. At the time, I discovered having a talent for creating imaginative stories. Together with Chuck Rapoport, we wrote Stalin, a six-hour miniseries for CBS Network Television. However, my heart was with fairytales. When my Hollywood experience was over, I was compelled to write *The Incredible Adventures of Kitto.* There was no planning, only a very strong conviction that I can and must do it, and a creative *Imagination.*

I had just finished *The Incredible Adventures of Kitto*, a beautifully illustrated trilogy of fairytale stories emphasizing to the young readers "every child is born to succeed". My income was quite low. Again, in my *Imagination,* I was visualizing large amounts of money deposited in my bank account with an unwavering conviction I have it. Indeed, this vision came through when all of a sudden I received an offer to produce Russian-American Investment Symposium in partnership with J. F. Kennedy School of Government, Harvard University. It was a Success.

Philippus Paracelsus, a famous Swiss alchemist, and physician, who lived in 14 century, was a great healer in his day. He stated that now is a scientific fact: "Whether the object of your faith is real or false, you will nevertheless obtain the same effects. Thus, if I believed in Saint Peter's stature as I should have believed in Saint Peter himself, I should obtain the same effects as I should have obtained from Saint Peter. That may be a superstition. Faith, however, produces miracles; and whether the subject of faith is true or false, it will always produce the same wonders. The cures attributed to the influence of certain relics are the effects of the people's *imagination* and confidence.

"We can easily conceive the marvelous effects which confidence and *imagination* can produce, particularly when both qualities are reciprocated between the subjects and the person who influences them."

Like most Russian people, we were poorer than a church mouse, and no one in Stalin's Russia would ever dream of traveling abroad. In 1945, it was as impossible as to travel to the moon. However, thanks to my mother, Emma, our neighbor, and my *Imagination*, I was traveling! At school, I was drawing tall ships under my command, at Emma's I was dying to get to another chapter of *Robinson Crusoe*, at night in my dreams I was fighting pirates or fighting together with them against

British navy. Several years later, my dream of travel has materialized.

Skepticism blocks creative process. People often believe only what they see. *Imagination* is nothing but fantasy to those who shuffle through life unaware of their great resource of *Imagination* and the mind's creativity. Remember Albert Einstein: *"Imagination is everything. It is a preview of life's coming attractions.*

Everyone who rose from rags to riches used *Imagination.* Despite their subconscious, like everyone else's, containing negativity, the necessary qualities of character, talent and powerful *Imagination*, as well as the absence of the negativity about the goal did the job. However, when there is no Love, negativity, mostly greed, takes over and become one's guide. The result is John D. Rockefeller, J. P. Morgan, Sheldon Adelson, etc.

When we take a good look at the creation, we see the World built with Love. Love is forever. We are created with Love and we are the Creators of Love. We use great gift of the *imagination* with Love, with gratitude, happily. Use it to benefit yourself, and everyone around you, and you would feel Happiness in every human being, in every blade of grass. Love, harmony, and Happiness are forever like beautiful flowers that never die.

To empower imagination, you may use some exercises. During concentration, imagine a goal being accomplished. It may be any goal like an event, your health, a new car or a house, anything. This exercise is suggested by the Russian psychic (as well as the member of the Russian Academy of Sciences) Georgy Grabovoi in his book

Live each present moment completely and the future will take care of itself.
Fully enjoy the wonder and beauty of each instant.

Methods of Concentration. This book provides concentrations methods for every day. I found these concentration methods highly beneficial as well as fun to exercise. Unfortunately, unlike some other Gregory's books, this one is not available in English.

Be open; listen to your intuition – the voice of Love. The effectiveness of these exercises, says Gregory, largely depends on you being accepting and loving. I wholeheartedly agree as I have tested some of them, effectively producing the envisioned results. Do not be surprised when in the process of concentration, you may obtain results of the goals you have envisioned in the past. You will know beforehand when this is in the process of happening and may cancel it if that goal is no longer necessary.

With this concentration method, you are contributing to the overall harmony and oneness of the world. You get more control over the events and circumstances you wish to create. In this exercise, you are concentrating on your right foot's sole that becomes a datum, a contact with and a reference point in the outside world. The earth in your imagination becomes a bearing point; at the same time, it is also a point of creation.

You recognize that if the earth creates everything that grows on it, that utilizing this truth, you may as effectively imagine and create any outward reality. This understanding is the essence of the exercise. However, during the exercise, you do not need to think about it because this creative mechanism works automatically and harmoniously when you are open to it and accept it. You may do this concentration several times a day for as long as you feel necessary.

In between concentrations, Gregory suggests focussing on your environment, imagining that every object in the outer world is an integral part of you and feel a light breeze coming from each object, gently caressing you. You realize that every object is a part of your consciousness and is in harmony with you and all other objects of the creation.

In another exercise concentrate on the elements that are in contact with your body. In the childhood, we learned that the sun, air, and water are our best friends. Now we want to comprehend our body's interaction with these friends.

Feel the warmth of the sun rays caressing your body. Feel a refreshing touch of the light breeze. It also could be strong gusts of wind or the air could be still and humid, and you would feel at the same time the warmth, the air, and the moisture on your cheeks. When swimming, you feel the water refreshing your body. With these contacts, you learn to interact consciously with the elements.

When during the concentration you are imagining/holding in mind your objective, whether it is an event, a circumstance or an object, it will materialize. Realize that harmony exists everywhere. It is also the harmony of change, of transformation. You know that you are contributing to the world's harmony and stability.

However, with the realization of Love, you will develop the most powerful *Imagination*.

103

There is another powerful creation method; I call it Infinite Archive of Love (IAL). It holds the thoughts and emotions of Love experienced by every human being since man became conscious.

It is an infinite pool of Love's tremendous benevolent power. IAL is the energy-informational organism of the higher order than individual consciousness. We can consciously access it and use this power to benefit ourselves, and the world. Of course, to use it, we must believe in the existence of the IAL beyond the shadow of the doubt.

It works. One of the reasons it works is because the mind can imagine, accept and become confident in any object of its choice, whether it is real or fantasy. When the mind thus convinces itself, this object, even when it was only imagined, becomes real to the mind and it can be used for any beneficial purpose, including the creation of the events, circumstances or objects of our choice. However, this reason is incidental. In case of the IAL, its reality is obvious because Love is not only our essence and a true substitute for a man-created term called soul, but it is also the essence of the creation, expressed in everything that exists on earth. Love feels the air as it is the essence in every living object from the blade of grass to sun and moon, to stars and galaxies, for the cosmos is made alive with Love. I am utilizing the IAL because I am convinced in the reality of it.

1. Make a simple pendulum to work with your subconscious. I use a little semiprecious stone with about 4" thread. With the pendulum, you may ask your subconscious any question that requires a

simple answer "Yes" or "Not." When pendulum moves horizontally, it means "No," vertically means "Yes."

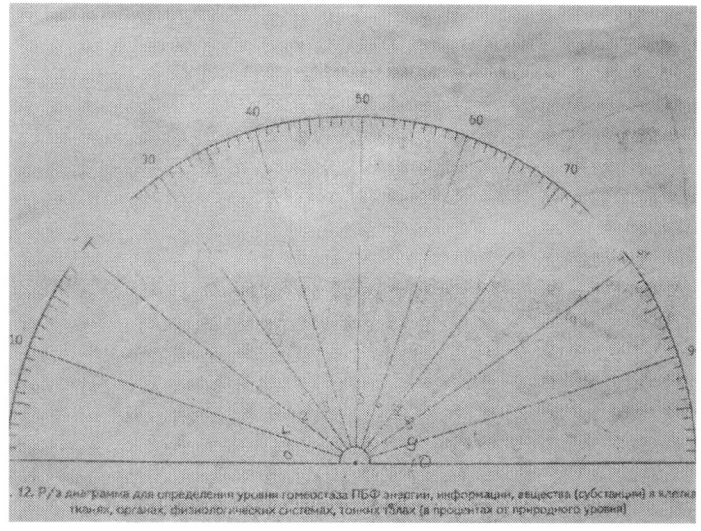

12. P/з диаграмма для определения уровня гомеостаза ПБФ энергии, информации, вещества (субстанции) в клетках, тканях, органах, физиологических системах, тонких телах (в процентах от природного уровня)

2.

Recreate this picture or print it (jpg) 8.5x11. It will enable you to test anything you wish and to find out if the object or relationship is good for you, including foods, books, tapes, teachers, seminars, cars, and so on.

3. Choose the book with poems of Love and Freedom. I use the Tao Te Ching translated by Gia-Fu Feng and Jane English. I have checked out several other additions of Tao Te Ching only to learn they are nearly not as good. Especially some later translations like the one by Stephen Mitchell, which is the worst.

4. Now choose the poem you wish to use and ask your pendulum if this poem is good for you to connect with AIL in order, for example, to restore your health: Yes or Not?

5. I am using # 33

> Knowing others is wisdom,
> Knowing the self is Enlightenment.
> Mastering others requires force;
> Mastering the self, needs strength.
>
> He who knows he has enough is rich.
> Perseverance is a sign of willpower.
> He, who stays where he is, endures.
> To die but not to perish is to be eternally present.

If the answer is 'Not', chose another poem and test it. I believe in this translation of Tao Te Ching any poem can be used. Still, you need to be sure your choice is appropriate.

Now ask your pendulum (over the drawing) how many times a day you have to read it to obtain the results you want. Use the drawing's numbers from 1 to 10 instead of 1 to 100.

In the same manner, ask how many times a day you need to repeat the poem (let us say it is 4). Then ask how many times you have to repeat it each time (let us say 6). Whenever you obtain the number, check it out for being correct, asking, "I need to repeat it six times, Yes, or Not?"

Now, memorize the poem and move on with it, knowing that the entire Infinite Archive of Love is backing you. Do not pray or beg, file in your request and start practicing. You may practice while exercising, walking, driving, cooking, whenever your mind is free.

Live each present moment completely and the future will take care of itself. Fully enjoy the wonder and beauty of each instant.

Blood of the Lion, an ancient city, lost in the Sahara Desert, Egypt

The Law of Happiness and Success

We are born to create instantly. Lester speaks of the three ways we can heal ourselves: spiritually, mentally or with the help of the doctors. Spiritual healing is instantaneous. An instantaneous creation can be executed to heal and create relationships, material goals, anything in our life. There is only one condition: our subconscious must be free of negativity – clean as a whistle. Thus, life bestows the *Transformation* upon us.

The law of Happiness and Success is written in stone and cannot be changed. People do not live by this law, because they are overwhelmed by ignorance with mental Conditioning and Resistance program barring them from the *Right Knowledge.* You are no exception. You are searching and searching without an end in view. You want Success, but you are sidetracked. The mind always is looking for an easy way, but there is no such thing as an "easy way," and, of course, the searching is easier than a serious practice. You must commit to either *Transformation* or *Classic meditation* or both. You must practice. Practice is everything. It is the only way to succeed.

According to the records, founded almost 3000 years ago, a city called *Blood of the Lion* prospered for almost thousand years. It became a well-known international seaport. Then, the sea moved away. A fleeting time of prosperity ended…, the *Blood of the Lion* was abandoned and disappeared, swallowed by the sands of the Sahara Desert. It was rediscovered only recently.

There were many prosperous cities in ancient time. However, there is no record of people living in these cities a life of Happiness. There was never a crowd that lived a life of Happiness. There were murderous, ignorant tribes bent on killing other people but no Happiness. Like Love and Freedom, Happiness was experienced only by a handful of individuals who decided to have a life of Happiness and found it.

Today we have information available on any aspect of life, Love, and Happiness; we have excellent communication tools. Still, there is no Love and Happiness in the human world because we have no time, we are afraid to lose, to be left behind, to be unsuccessful.... we are afraid. We live longer but waste time in spinning wheels and chasing shadows. If material progress is racing with ever-increasing speed, the human inner world is often at the Stone Age level. We are so ignorant we waste life on searching, but we have no time to practice. However, there is a good sign of the spiritual progress as well as more people come to understand the paramount importance of the inner grow at re-discovering Love and Happiness.

When researching some statistics for *The Lion Moves Alone,* I came across Andrew Carnegie's dictum. *He who dies rich dies disgraced.* It shocked me. Years before I had given up reading but now I was eagerly reading Carnegie's *Autobiography* and *The Gospel of Wealth.*

In *The Gospel of Wealth,* Carnegie appeals to the rich suggesting to give their wealth to services that would *benefit the nation and its people.* Andrew Carnegie was brought up in a loving family and was led by Love. His loving mind led him to give back to people his entire wealth of $320 billion. Without asking, he was rewarded with the most precious of all life's gifts: Happiness.

Ignorance is a king of the wealthy; greed is justified at any cost. "It is their money by law," says reader. True, but there is something else we have that is beyond the law of ignorance: Love. Only Love can lead one to share success and true Happiness. Love leads us to oneness and sharing. Meanwhile, Andrew Carnegie has been ceaselessly targeted with fake news by the wealthy and elite media. Does it matter when dogs bark?

In the thought that he (Ed. Andrew Carnegie) had worked for the realization of certain ideas, he discovered the secret of a serene and happy spirit, a characteristic which marked his life, especially after his retirement from business and up to the day of his death.   S.N.D. North

What can be more rewarding than Happiness and Success? *The Law of Happiness and Success* is pertinent to every field of life, every vocation when our endeavors are rooted in Love.

When several decades ago I experienced an out-of-body projection, it set me on the spiritual path of meditation, and yoga. I clearly defined my purpose: Freedom.

However, I also was making a living and had material goals to attain. This combination of the material path and spiritual often made me contemplate material success, causing an inquiry subtly to reside in the back of my mind: is there a rule that can be learned and applied, that will allow harnessing material success without losing spiritual goal of Freedom? Like most people, I believed material success is measured with money and desire for money thwarts inner growth. In my heart, I was convinced that there must be something like a formula of (true) Success and kept searching for it. When I "discovered" Andrew Carnegie, I knew I found it.

Andrew Carnegie demonstrated that when Success is created to benefit people, the creator will thrive as well as being gifted with Happiness. If Lester Levenson is a perfect example of how one finds Happiness with Love,

Andrew Carnegie is an enlightening example of how Love can harmonize Happiness and wealth. When you transform your negative subconscious past into Love, you will become another great example of the one who has caught two birds: Happiness and Success.

When there is no Love, there is no law of success; neither there are rules that help to create success. If there were rules, anyone would be able to learn how to create wealth. The Law of Success, which is taught to eager crowds, is a hoax created in a dreamland unaware (unintentionally). It is a dead-end road because it considers neither Love nor *Talent.* Blinded by desire people believe that studying and closely following those who have risen from rags to riches, they would become as successful… and fail.

Those who have risen from rags to riches themselves were never able to explain how they did it. Volumes have been written about how to become rich. However, there is no explanation of the mechanics of the process and no method. There are only hints, some common qualities of the character, etc., which means nothing because one unique thought makes a great deal of difference.

An unknown secret lies in uniqueness of an individual emotional-thinking process; in the intensity of thoughts; in a matchless thought pattern; as it is applied to a particular business; in the ability to influence and organize cooperation of the participants; in timing and circumstances of that time; in the ability to sense the right opportunity, as well as in many other unknowns, which altogether define *Talent* that is impossible to describe, never mind – recreate. The world is changing every instance, and there can be no two sets of the same circumstances or persons separated in time, except for the illusion of similarity created by the mind.

Love makes all the difference as it transforms a mythical law of success into powerful *The Law of Happiness and Success,* which is the law of Love. This law is true, and it can be learned and implemented.

"Nearly twenty years ago," writes Napoleon Hill in his *Law of Success,* "I interviewed Mr. Carnegie for the purpose of writing a story about him. During the interview, I asked him to what he attributed his success. With a merry little twinkle in his eyes, he said, *Young man before I answer your question will you please define your term 'success'.*

"After waiting until he saw that I was somewhat embarrassed by his request he continued: "By success, you have reference to my money, have you not?" I assured him that money was the term by which most people measured success, and he then said: "Oh, well if you wish to know how I got my money - if that is what you call success - I will answer your question by saying that we have a mastermind here in our business, and that mind is made up of more than a score of men who constitute my personal staff of superintendents and managers and accountants and chemists and other necessary types."

If you paid attention to the above, you would surely notice Carnegie's question "By success you have reference to my money, have you not?" This question should have led Hill to ask Carnegie what he, Carnegie, meant by success, but Hill failed to ask this most important of all questions.

Today, *The Giving People* is the most powerful demonstration of the humanity's inner growth as well as

The Law of Happiness and Success. Even like Carnegie, caring parents, who taught them integrity, brought up most of The Giving People, teaching them the value of giving that enabled them to live in the land of reality.

Gracious nature has not been sparing with her gifts. It bestowed Love upon every human being, with the ability to resolve every problem. The more loving the mind is, the more appropriate are our decisions.

The Law of Happiness and Success is simple to grasp as it means to be led by Love.

> The worldly hope men put their hearts upon
> Turns ashes or it prospers and anon,
> Like snow on dusty desert's face
> Lasting a little hour or two… is gone

Relatively a few people rose from rags to riches. Not guided by Love, they experienced much suffering, many troubles, exerted a great deal of effort. Most of them mercilessly exploited others and, all of them missed on Happiness. Every "captain of industry" went through this mill. This is what makes people believe that suffering is the necessary part of success. Wrong. Suffering is inevitable only in the absence of Love. Carnegie's life is the best proof of the great rise from rags to riches into an unparalleled Success that was created naturally, honestly, and with no suffering. *The Giving People* are following suit.

When Love is realized, *The Law of Happiness and Success* will guarantee Happiness, regardless of the size of income, which may be not so easy for some people to grasp. Every

Talent is different. When Love and Talent dictate for you to become a teacher, so be it. With Love and Talent, you will be a great teacher and will live a life of Happiness. Your Success will be expressed not in millions of dollars, but in fulfillment brought by being a wonderful teacher.

I have inherited this peculiarity and have often walked from the house to the gate intending to pull a flower for my buttonhole and then left for town unable to find one I could destroy.

Andrew Carnegie

Live each present moment completely and the future will take care of itself.
Fully enjoy the wonder and beauty of each instant.

The Needles. Sequoia National Forest, Southern California
(A view from my bedroom)

True dreamers of the American dream

George Washington, who often felt being guided by Love, said in his "Farewell Address":

"It will be worthy of a free, and enlightened, and at no distant period a great, nation to give to mankind the magnanimous and too novel example of a people always guided by an exalted justice and benevolence. Who can doubt that, in the course of time and things, the fruits of such a plan would richly repay any temporary advantages, which might be lost by a steady adherence to it? Can it be that Providence has not connected the permanent felicity of a nation with its virtue?"

When I tell others about *The Giving People,* I hear something like, 'millenniums of exploitation and abuse of the poor by the rich created a wall of mistrust.' However, now we have definite proof of honesty and responsibility.

Love and benevolence guided Andrew Carnegie. *The Gospel of Wealth* was published at the beginning of the last century. Carnegie believed the rich would follow in his steps; he was mistaken only in timing.

Today, as if celebrating a 100 anniversary of *The Gospel of Wealth* the *True Dreamers of the American Dream* are pledging their fortunes to the improvement of the people's well-being in the US and around the world. Indeed, *The Giving People* are being guided by Love, *an exalted justice, and benevolence.* Every member of this forum publicly pledged a major portion of wealth with some givers dedicating their entire assets to charitable causes.

Following are remarkable excerpts from the pledges. You will find complete pledges at TheGivingPeople.com. Every pledge is a revelation where you may discover sound ideas. You would learn that understanding, acceptance, and compassion lead every member of The Giving People initiative. A loving upbringing has been a major factor in shaping most of these people's personalities.

"In 2006, I made a commitment to gradually give all my Berkshire Hathaway stock to philanthropic foundations. I could not be happier with that decision. Now, Bill and Melinda Gates and I are asking hundreds of rich

Americans to pledge at least 50% of their wealth to charity. So, I think it is fitting that I reiterate my intentions and explain the thinking that lies behind them...

"...The reaction of my family and me to our extraordinary good fortune is not guilt, but rather a gratitude. Were we to use more than 1% of my claim checks on ourselves, neither our happiness nor well-being would be enhanced. In contrast, that remaining 99% can have a huge effect on the health and welfare of others. That reality sets an obvious course for me and my family: Keep all we can conceivably need and distribute the rest to society, for its needs. My pledge starts us down that course."

Warren Buffett

"...Our animating principle is that all lives have equal value. Put another way, it means that we believe every child deserves the chance to grow up, to dream and do big things. We have been blessed with good fortune beyond our wildest expectations, and we are profoundly grateful. But just as these gifts are great, so we feel a great responsibility to use them well. That is why we are so pleased to join in making an explicit commitment to the Giving Pledge."

Bill & Melinda Gates

"...My earliest memories include my father's exhortations about how important it is to give back. These early teachings were ingrained in me, and a portion of the first dollars I earned, I gave away. Over the years, the emotional and psychological returns I have earned from charitable giving have been enormous. The more I do for others, the happier I am. The happiness and optimism I have obtained from helping others are a big part of what keeps me sane."

Bill and Karen Ackman

"It is with a profound sense of relief that I am able to write this letter, expressing my intent to give away the vast majority of my wealth. Having the opportunity to help others achieve a better and more fulfilling life is not only an enormous privilege but also a lifelong dream. Several years ago, I received the support of my two young daughters, Jane and Hilary, in this pursuit. At an early age, my daughter, Jane, encouraged me to devote all of my resources to philanthropy and my dream of helping others. She assured me that my love and happiness were far more important to her than any inheritance she might receive."

Sue Ann Arnall

"About a decade ago I made a decision based on a destiny that had been defined 42 years previously. That decision was to start focusing much more on helping others in desperate need, rather than focusing on my own wealth creation. For this reason, along with the influence of other catalysts, I decided to sell my business, which I eventually did in 2006.

"About the same time, I decided that I was going to give at least half my wealth away when I died, as well as trying to change as many lives as possible during my lifetime. Part of this decision process was that I really don't think it is healthy and desirable for children to have such vast amounts of wealth left to them, and my philosophy is very much to encourage my children to forge their own success and happiness, even though that will undoubtedly involve much more modest levels of wealth creation."

John Caudwell

"Being a first generation American has many rewards. Among them is having the opportunity to succeed in this free country, and then succeeding enough to have the privilege of knowing that "success unshared is a failure." My mother raised my brother and me in a European immigrant community in downtown Los Angeles. From the time I was two years old, it was just the three of us. We didn't have very much, not even a TV; however, we did not realize that.

"One Christmas, when I was six years old, my mother took us to see the window displays and decorations in the big department stores in downtown Los Angeles. It was a big treat for us. We saw puppets that moved and trains that circled... It was really special and added to the Christmas spirit, but it didn't cost anything. That same year, my mother gave my brother and me a dime. She told both of us to hold half of it and put it in the bucket near a man who was ringing a bell. We did, and then we asked my mother why we gave him the dime (at the time, a dime could buy you three candy bars or two soda pops).

Live each present moment completely and the future will take care of itself.
Fully enjoy the wonder and beauty of each instant.

"My mom's reply was, "This is the Salvation Army that helps people who are really in need. Remember boys, no matter how much you have, there is always someone who is more in need than you. Always try to give, even if it is a little." Needless to say, that stuck with me in my adult life. Now my family and I have the privilege to help people and make the world a better place to live. This opportunity will not be passed up.

"Living is giving. I won't deprive my family of knowing how good it feels to help those in need with some of the basics we already have...food, shelter, care and a future. Whether it's feeding thousands of orphans in third world countries, saving whales, helping the homeless find employment, protecting our waterways, rescuing young girls from prostitution, teaching and supplying families in Appalachia with equipment to grow their own vegetables or any other worthwhile endeavor...giving back is a practice and joy I want my family to continue. I plan to help the world now and in the future — through my trust and my family — with half (if not more) of what I have been blessed with today. Peace, love and happiness: John Paul DeJoria Co-Founder John Paul Mitchell Systems Co-Founder Patron Spirits Company Co-Founder John Paul Pet Co-Founder ROK"

John Paul DeJoria

"The work of my life has been to develop software that would help keep people well and help sick people get better. It's been to create a system that allows us to discover the dangers of drugs like Thalidomide or Chloromycetin earlier before kids are harmed. It's to enable studies of data that bring us cures for cancer and resolve autism. It's to share information with other healthcare organizations wherever the patient goes.

Many years ago I asked my young children what two things they needed from their parents. They said 'food and money.' I told them 'roots and wings.' My goal in pledging 99% of my assets to philanthropy is to help others with roots—food, warmth, shelter, healthcare, education—so they too can have wings."

Judith R. Faulkner

"There is nothing more satisfying and exciting than being able to positively affect people and noble causes in this world. We are fortunate to be in the position to join the Giving Pledge and state publicly that the majority of our wealth will be contributed to philanthropy during our lifetimes or after we leave this world.

This was an easy decision for us. We have both been involved with non-profit causes for many years."

Dan and Jennifer Gilbert

"From a young age, my brothers and I were taught to give to those less fortunate than ourselves, no matter how little we had. That ethos has remained at the core of our family since childhood and, today, thanks to my business success, I am very fortunate to be able to help many thousands of women and children in Africa. It is so important that those of us who have enjoyed fortune in business utilize our skills and knowledge in philanthropy to empower people to help themselves. Through my Foundations, I hope to continue to contribute to improving the lives of women and children for many years to come and I am honored to join the Giving Pledge."

Ann Gloag OBE

"My Charitable Giving Plan. It has been clear to me since my earliest childhood memories that my reason for being was to help others. The desire to give back was the impetus for pursuing an education in business, for applying that education to founding what became a successful container company, and for using that experience to grow our differentiated chemicals corporation into the global enterprise it has become. The journey which began in poverty somehow led to my name's inclusion on the Richest Americans list for several years running."

John and Karen Huntsman

"I suppose I arrived at my charitable commitment largely through guilt. I recognized early on, that my good fortune was not due to superior personal character or initiative so much as it was to dumb luck. I was blessed to be born in an advanced society with caring parents. So, I had the advantage of both genetics (winning the "ovarian lottery") and upbringing.

"As I looked around at those who did not have these advantages, it became clear to me that I had a moral obligation to direct my resources to help right that balance. America's "social contract" is equal opportunity. It is the most fundamental principle in our founding documents and it is what originally distinguished us from the old Europe. Yet, we have failed in achieving that seminal goal; in fact, we have lost ground in recent years.

"Another distinctly American principle is a shared partnership between the public and private sectors to foster the public good. So, if the democratically-directed public sector is shirking, to some degree, its responsibility to level the playing field, more of that role must shift to the private sector. As I addressed my charitable purposes, all of this seemed pretty clear: I was only peripherally responsible for my own good fortune; I was moral duty bound to help those left behind by the accident of birth; America's root principle was an equal opportunity but we were far from achieving it."

George B. Kaiser

"Dear Warren: I have responded affirmatively to the Giving Pledge. In fact, I have fulfilled that pledge already, having given more than half my wealth to charitable causes, primarily cancer research. I have also committed, and reaffirm here, that the balance of my estate — other than what is needed to support my wife during her lifetime — will also be given to charity. My thinking is rather simple: I learned as a young boy that sharing with others is the right thing to do, a lesson I observed from my father's willingness to share even our meager means with those less fortunate. Ever since it has never been difficult for me to continue to do the right thing. I trust your efforts in growing the ranks of those committed to the Giving Pledge will be matched by the effort to see those pledges fulfilled. Thank you for your leadership. Warmest Regards,"

Sidney Kimmel.

"Nancy and I are inspired by the leadership of the Giving Pledge. Fourteen years ago, when we set up our personal foundation and committed to giving 95% of our wealth to charitable causes either during our lifetimes or at our deaths, we never dreamed that there would be such a gathering of like-minded individuals who firmly believe in the favorable impact of giving to the world.

"Our home community in Houston. As longtime residents of this city, we have witnessed its extraordinary culture of entrepreneurship, which has enabled Houstonians of all backgrounds to improve their lives, use their talents and creativity, and pursue their dreams. In Houston, you are what you achieve. This stirs and motivates us to continue giving. The Kinder Foundation's mission is to enable our community to flourish by providing Transformational gifts to projects dedicated primarily to three key areas: urban green space, education, and quality of life issues.

"Nancy and I grew up in small towns and firmly believe in the opportunity for entrepreneurship in America and especially in Houston and we believe in giving back to society the bulk of the good fortune we have received. Our goal in joining the Giving Pledge is to encourage those in similar positions to do the same."

Rich and Nancy Kinder

"We have an opportunity and an obligation to prepare our children for the real world, for dealing with others in practical, project-based environments. It is about working together and building character — being compassionate, empathetic, and civil as a means to a greater end. As technology changes, so do students. So should classrooms, and so should our methods of teaching. In a few short years, connectivity has gone from a technological novelty to a daily necessity. It is how our culture communicates, and our children are at the forefront of its use.

"Understanding those tools — and how to integrate them into learning — is an integral step in defining our future. My pledge is to the process; as long as I have the resources at my disposal, I will seek to raise the bar for future generations of students of all ages. I am dedicating the majority of my wealth to improving education. It is the key to the survival of the human race. We have to plan for our collective future — and the first step begins with the social, emotional, and intellectual tools we provide to our children.

"As humans, our greatest tool for survival is our ability to think and to adapt — as educators, storytellers, and communicators our responsibility is to continue to do so."

George Lucas and Mellody Hobson

"I too believe that all our efforts in creating the wealth that we have would give us a great deal more joy if we were to disperse as much of it during our lifetimes. We've been focused on this work at The Marcus Foundation since our conversation many years ago. For example, The Georgia

Aquarium, which is the largest in the world, has given over 12 million visitors the joy of seeing fish and mammals that the overwhelming majority would have never had the opportunity to see in their lifetime.

"It also helped stimulate our downtown economy offering jobs and new opportunities. The work we do with hospitals, education, and children through the Marcus Autism Center (MAC), has enabled us to take care of well over 36,000 children since its inception and approximately 4,000 children annually. If it weren't for the MAC in Georgia there would be nowhere for many of these families to go. I share this with you because of happiness one can conceive by watching the joys of their work."

Bernie and Billi Marcus

"Dear Warren, Bill, and Melinda, We've long embraced the principles of The Giving Pledge. Charity is something we learned at an early age, whether during grade school riding our bikes around the neighborhood collecting dimes and quarters for the American Cancer Society, or later, participating in community service programs in high school. From the time we began formal philanthropic programs in the 1970s, we've made contributions at a rate that will assure distribution of the overwhelming majority of assets during our lifetimes.

"The charitable programs we began when we were in our early 30s to advance education and progress against life-threatening diseases were later formalized with the launch of our family foundations in 1982. Our goal has been to discover and advance inventive and effective ways of helping people help themselves and those around them to lead productive and satisfying lives. We do that primarily through our work in education and medical research."

Michael and Lori Milken

"Among the Giving Pledge partners, of course, we have different circumstances and specific thinking around the motivation for joining. In my case, many years ago I formally and privately committed more than 50% of my net worth to philanthropic causes. The issue for me then was the public disclosure of the Giving Pledge. In the end, I came to the view that by openly joining other Pledge partners I might encourage others to follow. This thought makes disclosure compelling.

"One of the admirable qualities of our great country is the history and culture of helping those less fortunate. In America giving is not unusual; it is mainstream. I always thought if I were lucky enough to be in a position to help others, I would. The vast majority of Americans are this way. This is who we are. And while separate acts of generosity are generally not remarkable, taken as a whole, it defines us. I never imagined not doing my part.

"I have been lucky in two significant ways. First, I had the good luck to be raised by parents who provided me with an education, good values, and love. In other words, the odds of leading a productive life were materially tilted in my favor. Second, fortune smiled on me in my work over the past thirty years. I do work hard (probably too hard), but others have worked harder and smarter with less financial success."

Jonathan M. Nelson

"I am very pleased to pledge that I plan to contribute the substantial majority of my assets to philanthropy. I am well on my way. I do so with great pleasure. And for several reasons. My parents were Greek immigrants who came to America at age 17, with 3rd-grade education, not a word of English and hardly a penny in their pockets. Their dream was the American dream, not just for themselves but for their children as well. My father took a job no one else would take — washing dishes in a steamy caboose on the Union Pacific railroad.

"He ate and slept there and saved virtually every penny he made. He took those savings and started the inevitable Greek restaurant, open 24 hours a day for 365 days a year for 25 years. Throughout this period, he always sent money to his desperately poor family in Greece and fed countless numbers of hungry poor who came knocking on the back door of his restaurant. Above all else, he wanted to save so as to invest in his children's education.

"As I watched and learned from my father's example, I noticed how much pleasure his giving to others gave him. Indeed, today, I get much more pleasure giving money to what I consider worthwhile causes than making the money in the first place. As I checked with other philanthropists, I found this was a very common experience. For example, I have been particularly pleased to support causes and institutions for which I have a passion and for which I contribute myself, that is my personal capital, as well as my financial capital."

Peter G. Peterson

"We are among the converted having committed to giving all our net worth to philanthropy starting with a grant of $1.3 billion in 2006 to our spend-down Foundation. When you think about it, no other approach seems to make sense. Passing down fortunes from generation to generation can do irreparable harm. In addition, there is no way to spend a fortune. How many residences, automobiles, airplanes and other luxury items can one acquire and use?

"The Buffett/Gates initiative is likely to be a major "game changer." Their partnership and dedication and their challenge to billionaires to share their wealth with the less fortunate will undoubtedly unlock a substantial amount of funds. Congratulations! As former CEOs of a highly successful financial institution, we were rewarded monetarily beyond our wildest imagination, at the same time experiencing the emotional high associated with building a great company from scratch and winning in the competitive race."

Herb and Marion Sandler

"I grew up in a middle-class family in Canada. My dream was to be a writer who tells stories that make a difference in the world. Along the way, when I got out of business school, I became the first full-time employee and the first President of a fledgling company with an online auction service called AuctionWeb. That company later became better known by its corporate name, eBay. When the company went public in 1998, all of a sudden I went from being in debt and living in a house with five roommates, to having hundreds of millions of dollars in the value of my eBay shares.

"Until then, I had not thought much about philanthropy. But with my newfound paper wealth, I resolved to do good things for the world with that money, in smart ways. The first thing I did, in 1999, was to start the Skoll Foundation. Today, the Skoll Foundation has become the leading organization in the world supporting social entrepreneurs to drive large-scale impact. Each year, we find innovative social entrepreneurs from around the world — people like Paul Farmer of Partners in Health or Ann Cotton of Camfed — and we support them over a multiyear period."

Jeff Skoll

"There has existed in the minds of refugees, who have been embraced by this great country, a level of gratitude for the opportunities made available to us that is somewhat analogous to a debt that we feel needs to be repaid. Some of us refer to that feeling as wanting to "give back" — I personally prefer to call it wanting to "share opportunity". And in terms of the time, energy, and money already contributed by me to replicate such an opportunity for others, my family and I have already more than fulfilled the intent of the Giving Pledge."

Tad Taube

Live each present moment completely and the future will take care of itself.
Fully enjoy the wonder and beauty of each instant.

"Giving back was instilled in me by my father at a young age. In addition to being active with Rotary and other civic organizations, my dad was also philanthropic with his own small resources. Not only did he make contributions to causes that he cared about, he also supported the tuition of two African American students at his alma mater, Millsap's College in the late 1950s. It made a big impression on me to see someone as hard-charging as my father take the time to quietly help out two young people like this."

Ted Turner

"By any possible measure, I have had an extraordinarily fortunate life (and a long one) for which I am very grateful. I couldn't be more thankful for the life I have been lucky enough to live in the best country in the world. If I didn't have ten bucks in the bank, I would still feel this way. I have been so fortunate in my professional life that I want to give it back to society in a meaningful way. So, I'm happy to sign on to the Giving Pledge, because every one of us has the opportunity — and the obligation — to make a difference by helping other people."

"Unfortunately, there remain more than 40 million people who have lost their sight needlessly and those numbers are going up at an alarming rate. Half of them are blinded by untreated cataracts. In many regions of the developing world, 60-70% of all blindness is cataract-related. In addition, there are close to two hundred million who are visually impaired by cataract disease leading unfulfilled lives. This is all happening in spite of the existence of a miracle surgery called Manual Small Incision Cataract

Surgery (MSICS) which takes as little as 5 minutes to perform and costs as little as $35.

"With the encouragement of my son, Jim, we founded a not-for-profit organization called HelpMeSee. Its purpose is to promote MSICS and deliver a high fidelity simulator-based training system to train 30 thousand highly skilled MSICS specialists. We have assembled a wonderful team of medical, simulator engineering, instructional courseware designers, management, development, and financial experts. I am personally committed to validating the efficacy of high fidelity simulator training of Manual Small Incision Cataract Surgery (MSICS)."

Albert Lee Ueltschi

"I have been fortunate that I grew up in a family where charity was ingrained in us from a very early age. We were immigrants to a new country, Dubai, United Arab Emirates. Even, when my father earned a small amount, a large percentage was shared with the community we lived in, sometimes at the cost of our own comfort. To this day, our underlying philosophy remains that good giving 'pinches,' meaning that the sacrifice you make, has to be felt, else, the act remains just another financial transaction in our lives; and therein lies the appeal of the Giving Pledge to us. I was also lucky that my parents were school teachers. They always placed a great emphasis on the value of education. While perhaps I didn't live up to their expectations as a student, I saw the impact they had on people's lives. I have always believed that education is key to fixing so many of the world's greatest problems: violence, poverty, and health. It all starts with education.

Live each present moment completely and the future will take care of itself.
Fully enjoy the wonder and beauty of each instant.

These two pillars of charity and education have always guided me, and out of them came the Varkey Foundation, to change lives through education around the world.

"We, particularly, focus on capacity building interventions for teachers and school leaders and championing their work through initiatives such as the Global Teacher Prize. Everyone deserves a great teacher. Through the Giving Pledge, we hope to take these efforts to a greater level."

Sunny & Sherly Varkey

These are examples of understanding and compassion practiced by *The Giving People*, talented creators of wealth. Many millions of other talents will not create wealth even when led by Love. Nevertheless, when led by Love, every talent must result in Happiness and Success.

Could compassion and wealth sharing eliminate inequality? 50 years ago, this issue was out of the question, but today *The Giving People* are proving it is achievable. When only one-half of all the rich persons in America join *The Giving People,* inequality will begin fading out. With 90% of all American rich joining *The Giving People* inequality will cease to exist. It is not just because of the sharing but mostly because the talented American financial minds will be forever generating ever more wealth with a major part of it supporting social needs.

"Though almost all of us grew up believing in the concept of equal opportunity, most of us simultaneously carried the unspoken and inconsistent "dirty little secret" that genetics drove much of accomplishment so that equality was not achievable." George B. Kaiser/*The Giving people*

Genetics and talent contribute to the *accomplishment* of the financial goals. *The Giving People* also contribute to equality. *The Giving People* offered their solution to inequality. They understand that together with the talent to create wealth comes the responsibility to share it with "the poorer brethren". It is the same solution as the one offered by Andrew Carnegie in *The Gospel of Wealth*:

This, then, is held to be the duty of the man of wealth: To set an example of modest, unostentatious living, shunning display or extravagance; to provide moderately for the legitimate wants of those dependent upon him; and, after doing so, to consider all surplus revenues which come to him simply as trust funds, which he is called upon to administer, and strictly bound as a matter of duty to administer in the manner which, in his judgment, is best calculated to produce the most beneficial results for the community – the man of wealth thus becoming the mere trustee and agent for his poorer brethren, bringing to their service his superior wisdom, experience, and ability to administer, doing for them better than they would or could do for themselves.

You may notice that *The Giving People* are rarely using the word Love in their pledges, yet their charitable decisions are motivated by the sense of responsibility, compassion, and kindness..., which is Love. They are true dreamers of the American Dream living to the fullest, for nothing is as fulfilling as opportunities created to help others.

Live each present moment completely and the future will take care of itself.
Fully enjoy the wonder and beauty of each instant.

I wish to conclude this chapter with a story of Love and Success featuring an average businessperson who was brought up with Love.

My friends Fritzie and Jerry (right)

Jerry's natural loving attitude paved his way to success in his native Canada and the USSR. Love banished the Soviet authorities' doubts and suspicion; it removed all restrictions to Success in Jerry's way. Jerry's life is a graphic example of Love giving us all we need.

Jerry owned a small ad agency with offices in Montreal and Toronto. When he came to Moscow, I was assigned to make for him a documentary *Children of the USSR*. In this documentary, the Russian children were filmed wearing clothing produced by Monsanto that was Jerry's account.

135

Back home, as it was customary, Jerry sent the documentary to every television network in the US and Canada. That year an annual baseball game was delayed. A producer at the ABC Network Television that was broadcasting the game took from the shelf *Children of the USSR*, an exotic subject at the time. The documentary was run worldwide to fill the time gap. It was phenomenal free exposure for Monsanto that otherwise would have to pay to ABC a huge amount of money to run it as an ad.

It was not the end of the story, however, as there also were raving reviews of the film in major newspapers in the US and Canada. Monsanto was delighted. When at the age of 75 Jerry retired, Monsanto kept him as a consultant for another 12 years.

Even like Andrew Carnegie, Jerry was always brought in contact with good people. His staff was a pleasure to work with. Most of the employees stay with Jerry until his retirement. Like Carnegie, Jerry was not competing. Only in the beginning, he was soliciting business. Once the company was established, clients had lined up at the door of his agency. Being so successful, Gerry was often offered to expand his agency, but he preferred to keep it small. "It is more enjoyable to manage," he said, "and it lets me spend more time with my wife and children."

When Love is our natural state, all superficialities fade away. Religious, cultural, social, racial differences and barriers disappear, and people of opposite ideologies come to a mutual understanding on any subject as the power of Love lifts them beyond artificial differences created in ignorance.

Like Andrew Carnegie, Jerry was brought up in a poor but truly loving home. He was a kind, straightforward, and sincere person. I saw that Jerry's wife Fritzie supported all his undertakings. They live happily together for over 65 years.

When I left the USSR, Jerry and Fritzie came down to visit me in Israel, the only place where the Soviets allowed immigration at the time. Later I came to Canada, bought used New Yorker, a car of my dream – the largest car at the time☺, started my own production company and shot some jingles and documentaries for Jerry and other clients. I had an ample time to watch Jerry at home and work. I never saw Jerry getting angry, irritated or raising his voice. I was envious of his calm and loving personality.

Transformation is a simple method, yet it requires your full co-operation. Every human being possesses Love, usually hidden under a pile of dross. It means every human being has the ability to discover it anew. The time necessary for this discovery would vary depending on different factors. One of these factors is age and amount of accumulated negativity hidden in the subconscious. Another – your determination and the intensity in the *Transformation* process....

We are born with Love, and if we "lost" it, we could discover it anew. When someone is saying, "*Transformation* is not for me," this is an excuse because Love is universal and is present in everyone – a beautiful and powerful state waiting for you to discover☺

Live each present moment completely and the future will take care of itself.
Fully enjoy the wonder and beauty of each instant.

Ancient Lake Quaroun (from the Sahara Desert)

Addendum

Subconscious

The moving finger writes; and, having writ,
Moves on: nor all thy piety nor wit
Shall lure it back to cancel half a line,
Nor all thy tears wash out a word of it.

"…thy tears" will not wash it out, only the *Transformation*
will. Besides regulating bodily processes and instincts, the
subconscious serves as an archive of the events that take
place in our life as well as our every emotional experience.

The archival part of the subconscious contains everything we have learned and accepted to be true or a lie, real or false, good or bad. Many past negative events are forgotten by the conscious mind yet; the subconscious is keeping their records forever. It is this archival part of the subconscious that needs to be freed from its negative content.

Whatever your position in life at the moment, it has resulted from your subconscious' miraculous ability to exert a pull at and attract things and circumstances your mind has been dwelling upon. It is a general rule. Genetic information may overrule this concept. There may be other exceptions to this rule. However, opposite thoughts of doubts, fears, etc., supported by corresponding feelings, as well as long forgotten concepts contrary to your purpose would obstruct or may destroy your positive intentions. It is forever happening in an average person's mind. A chaotic ETP (Emotional Thinking Process) filled with doubts, "I can't," fears and regrets are unceasingly "downloaded" in the subconscious and create a chaotic life.

The subconscious cannot be controlled, but it can be cleansed. You can learn to control ETP. You can also learn what to program in the subconscious. You will begin to gain more control as soon as you start the *Transformation process.* It is not difficult, but you must make a decision – an irrevocable decision to do it and act upon it. Lack of making the decision and acting upon it creates armies of procrastinators.

Tomorrow you will also have to decide. Why not today? Tomorrow you will get neither younger no wiser. Tomorrow may never come. Then, make the decision now. When you begin removing the impediments, your confidence will mature, and you will be able to steer your life in the desired direction.

Time is of the essence. Life flies. You cannot afford to waste your life, for this great gift is given to us only once, unless humanity will become so advanced that by the year 3000 it will be able to raise the dead. However, that is a long time to wait for. Use every instant of this wonder called life to gain Happiness and Success. The decision means an action that instantly elevates you beyond time. As soon as you make this most important decision, you kill procrastination, you are off and flying into a life so beautiful, the words can hardly describe.

Live each present moment completely and the future will take care of itself.
Fully enjoy the wonder and beauty of each instant.

Classic Meditation™

With rare exceptions, every enlightened being found Freedom with Classic Meditation or *Transformation*™

It was only one Buddha... after his death, the followers created 32 different schools of Buddhism. It was only one enlightened Buddha, who taught Love and Classic Meditation. Unenlightened followers had to interpret it in 32 different ways.

It was only one Lester Levenson, who formulated Releasing technique and demonstrated how to find Love with the *Transformation process*. After his passing, Lester's associates created several Releasing Technique

141

classes. But it is not as simple anymore. Lester did not charge his students money. The instructors encapsulated Lester's teaching into expensive CDs, books, and seminars. Lester realized Love and Freedom by using *Transformation* exclusively. The teachers do not offer the *Transformation* to the students.

For millennia, people were practicing Classic Meditation to find Love and Freedom. Today, using bits and pieces of Classic Meditation some teachers created different types of meditation techniques that may help you to a temporary relaxation but will never help to the realization of Love and a permanent state of peace. Mio Clinic, for example, describes meditation thus:

"During meditation, you focus your attention and eliminate the stream of jumbled thoughts that may be crowding your mind and causing stress." This ignorant and misleading information demonstrates lack of *the Right Knowledge*. In meditation, we focus on nothing. All we do is watching our thoughts and emotions without reacting. The innovations are created by the egos. They are of a very little help even in daily life; they are impotent at the realization of Love and Peace.

"There is no better medicine than (Classic) Meditation, that would help open your eyes," says Osho. "Words medicine and meditation both have the same root; both words mean the same. Medicine treats your body and Meditation is treating your mind. Medicine is treating your outer form and meditation – your inner being."

Meditation is actually treating both your mind and body, for when mind is healthy, body will heal as if by itself, without medicine, as it was demonstrated by Lester. Both *Transformation* and meditation have no side effects but a great number of benefits☺ and there is no need for a teacher. Practice! It is all you need.

Classic Meditation is a simple and the most effective way to Love and Freedom. It also would require more time than *Transformation*. However, meditation is a more powerful tool because it gifts you with Samadhi and supreme Freedom. Keep it simple. Discard all complications such as the Chakras theory, Kundalini, and all other eastern attachments. All you need is practice.

Unless after several sessions you fall in love with meditation, do not force yourself just for the sake of doing it or because someone says, it is a great thing to do. There is a big difference between forcing and disciplining oneself. Discipline is necessary for any practice while forcing is always wrong. There is also a fine line between disciplining and forcing… do not step over it.

Because there is no (direct) connection between the state of Freedom and an average mental state (when Love does not lead us), people are often substituting Classing meditation with surrogates – "quickies" that are of a little benefit. Today practice of the Classic meditation is corrupted even damaged with alterations. As one keeps mastering Classic meditation, positive mental changes become apparent and encouraging. Consequently, positive changes also take place in one's life.

You know, my friends, how long since in my house
For new marriage I did make carouse:
Divorced old barren reason from my bed,
And took the daughter of the vine to spouse.

Barren reason: dogmatic knowledge. The daughter of the vine: meditation.

Meditation is seating still in a comfortable posture and witnessing the mind without reacting to it. This leads to a total suspension of the emotional thinking process as well as purging the subconscious of its negative and conceptual past. When this stage of the mind's emptiness is reached, you will be hinted as to what to do next. If anything☺.

Some teachers suggest that Samadhi is the realization of the soul. To me it is the realization of Love, then great Peace, and then, after the successful session, – back to the state of Love in daily life.

Symbolically, the goal of mediation is Samadhi, a breathless state of the unencumbered piece yet, in reality, meditation has no goal; it is a beautiful experience. Samadhi also bestows Love upon us and brings an understanding of life in its wholeness, when life is no longer fragmented by the mind when it is a reality beyond the 'good' and "bad." When you meditate deeply and keep increasing length of the sessions, even if you do not experience Samadhi, meditation will dramatically improve your life.

Expectations are necessary. When not in session imagine being at peace when nothing can disturb you. In the session, we expect nothing, feel nothing, and think of nothing. We are a witness to the mind, thoughts, and emotions and then… "We" seize to exist in an inexplicable state of unencumbered peace when the mind is moved beyond its limitations, beyond common sense and logic, beyond Love and wisdom.

Repetition of mantra, chanting, concentration is not meditation. These techniques would only temporarily calm the mind, helping to prepare it for the meditation.

Mantras have no power that is often ascribed to them. The power may be generated only by you. The mantra is an aid to meditation. We may start meditation session with a mantra in order initially to calm the mind. As the mind is getting calmer, it is also easier to watch. For a mantra to become a useful aid to meditation and/or *Transformation,* it must be rooted in Love. You must believe unconditionally in the meaning you ascribe to the mantra.

The first step in meditation (and the last☺) is to learn to witness the mind's movement, no matter where it goes. When this step is mastered, the rest of your journey to Samadhi will happen as if by itself providing you would escalate the intensity and the length of your sessions. A maximum amount of time I spent in meditation was nine hours; after that, I did not have to increase it any longer.

Take a note: both methods *Transformation* and Classic meditation have a common ingredient. *Watching the mind* is the main practice in both methods. Of course, the realization of Love takes place in both cases, *Transformation* and Classic meditation. However, only with mastering *watching the mind,* we would realize Love and experience Samadhi.

Silence reached with the help of thought is not useful. Silence reached through realizing the source of the thought is great. When thought becomes aware of its source, when it realizes that it is never free and is always old, then silence will come. It happens when we master witnessing of the mind.

When we can be fully aware of the mind while watching a movie without either judging or losing ourselves in it – this is almost meditation. Impartial witnessing our surroundings and ourselves is a great practice that may be performed anywhere, anytime. These are useful techniques but not yet meditation. Meditation is a state of the whole mind not contaminated by thought or emotion. Meditation does not have a particular technique or an authority. It is probably the most beautiful of life's arts. It is not a physical culture; it is wisdom that comes extended to our everyday life.

The mind uncontrolled and unguided will drag us down, down forever. It will render us, kill us, while the mind controlled and guided will save us, free us, said Vivekananda. He was a foremost mediator and the first spiritual ambassador to the US from India.

At the beginning of my meditation sessions, I could not sit quietly even for a few minutes. Everything was calling to my attention, provoking thoughts and action. All else would suddenly become very important. The false sense of importance was created by the mind. Decide to meditate and begin with a session of three minutes long.

Before meditation take a 10 - 15-minute walk or do a simple physical or breathing exercise.

Find a spot where you will not be disturbed. Ventilate the room and keep it cool. Place a small cushion on top of the seat of the chair and a woolen rug on top of the cushion. The lower part of the rug should be long enough for your feet to place over it. The wool is used to prevent the energy from escaping. You may come up with some other means helping to contain energy. Cover your shoulders with a sweater when cold. Sit in a yoga posture on a chair or cushion in a manner as comfortable as possible, wear loose clothing.

This is the site four the yoga postures: https://www.yogaindailylife.org/system/en/exercise-levels/sitting-postures-for-pranayama-and-meditation.

Padma Sana – Lotus posture is the best. If you are physically impaired, choose a simpler posture from this site. Start Practicing. Do not waste your time looking for something else.

Relax....

Keep your spine straight without straining, your chin — parallel to the floor. Hold your body straight without leaning to the left or right, forward or backward. Your ears should be in alignment with your shoulders, and your nose in a straight line with your navel. Keep the tongue touching the roof of the mouth and close your lips. Eyes are closed or slightly open, and breathing is quiet through the nose.

Breathe with your stomach. When inhaling, do not lock your breath within but hold it with a sustained force of inhalation and stomach muscles.

Place your hands on top of thighs with palms facing up, small fingers touching the lower abdomen. Get used to the pose of sitting comfortably. When using a chair (only when you cannot practice with one of the Yoga postures), above do not touch the back of the chair with your back. Do not put any support between your back and the back of the chair. From the very start, learn to sit straight without any support.

Physically I am an ordinary person, and I learned to meditate with a group for two hours and longer without intermission, for intermissions are disturbing the process. People use something to support their back, get up every 45 minutes, etc. You can do it right from the very start and without breaks. Just decide to do it right and do it. There is nothing difficult about it, but when the mind is not prepared, it may try to find excuses. Educate it with the right knowledge, make it your friend and it will co-operate. SRF offers free meditation classes in their beautiful temple at the Lake Shrine, Santa Monica. They meditation facilities free at many locations throughout the US.

Before you begin a session, take several slow, deep breaths. Hold your body erect, allowing your breathing to become normal again. Do not follow your breath, do not fix your thoughts on forms or colors, do not fix your thoughts on space, gods, angels…. Do not fix your thoughts on what you ever saw, heard or memorized. Just

Live each present moment completely and the future will take care of itself.
Fully enjoy the wonder and beauty of each instant.

witness the thoughts as they come and go. When out of session, expect to be free; it is helpful to imagine yourself in a state of peace. Keep these expectations in the back of your mind.

During the session imagination and recollection must be excluded from the mind.

Do not strain. Do not ask questions. Just follow the procedure. The mind loves questioning. Do not let it find any excuse to distract you. Time will come, and there will be the answer to your every question. Be patient. Most of your questions will drop away as unimportant.
Force nothing. Be persistent, patient and alert. Do not try to make anything happen.... let meditation happen to you. Always persevere a little longer, be an extra patient. That is the only effort you use.

You are learning how to watch your mind peacefully, how to be a witness.

Feel your spine and, from time to time, very subtly straighten it, 'pool' it up without strain. It must be a very gentle feeling, like a feather flying....

If in the beginning, we are witnessing conscious mind, down the road we may come to witness the deeper recesses of our subconscious, an archive holding our every experience. In *Transformation* we are converting our subconscious negative past into Love. When the past subconscious event would surface in meditation, we do nothing but witnessing it as we would witness a landscape.

Inexplicably, our negative past is cleansed more with every session.

When Samadhi happens, the entire negative archive is dissolved with some other positive alterations caused by the genes being turned on and off. It is similar to *The Momentum of Love* that we experience in *Transformation*. We know that we think, but we do not know how thoughts happen. We identify with the content of the thought and allow ourselves to be disturbed by it. When emotions and thoughts arise during meditation, remember that everything we have in the mind was put there by ourselves. Influence of the negative subconscious content handicaps us most. Practicing witnessing the mind, we learn not to follow our thoughts and emotions or react in any way as if we are watching it I happening to someone else. We also learn through this process how to deal with problems. Being at peace, we would allow the right solution to come in sooner.

Watch your mind. Many thoughts will crowd there; watch them sailing infinitely through your mind. In the beginning, trains of thoughts will consistently run through your mind. We do not identify with their content or feel that it is part of us. There is something in us, an identity, which is distinct and separate from this mental content. When in deeper meditation our senses are shut, we have an even greater sense of identity, a sense of self, which is Love. We learn to witness the train, knowing it is not us, but a product of our making.

Everything in our mind belongs to that mental train. We need only to observe it, even when in the beginning it is not clear where the train comes from and where it goes. We learn to never suppress or struggle with our thoughts and never argue with anything on that train. We witness it and let pass without identifying with it. When the train continues to linger, we simply watch it for as long as necessary, as if we are sitting in the car at the intersection, waiting for some train to rumble by…. Eventually, it has to pass and disappear. Then, when a stray thought crosses a blue nothingness of our mind, we watch it go.

Whatever is our experience in meditation, we are not attached to it and not trying to stop, delay, repeat or get rid of it. We will treat every experience as we treat a thought: be aware of it and witnessing it coming and going. When one is free, there are no thoughts in meditation and no experiences. Awareness is experiencing itself.

At the beginning of the session, if it is too difficult to watch thoughts and emotions, you may use the following techniques:

- become aware of the spot between the eyebrows, or
- employ a single thought, like "What am I," or
- watch your breath.

Another technique is called Expanded Awareness. Become aware of the point about one half of the meter above your head. Stay there for a few minutes. Then, with every inhalation enlarge your presence and move beyond the body. Become aware of expanding it beyond the room, house, and street, including a town, a country, the globe, the universe and the worlds beyond.... sensing it all within yourself. I use this technique after mind gets quite relaxed. It is not meditation, but the techniques may be helpful, providing we use it in the very beginning and for just a few minutes.

There is another technique. Imagine yourself in a meditative posture levitating just a few inches above the top of your head. Concentrate on being there. Watch your mind in this position. That is all. Simple, is it not? It may be a little more involving, but it is also more rewarding. Try it☺

Watch your body for any movement: the body must be still. I learned that the above techniques help to still the body sooner. As soon as the body gets still, I would drop the assistance and begin watching the mind. It is also possible to discover some means of your own that will help you to still the body.

Truth is perfect and complete. It is present in the process of watching the mind, as well as in our every experience. Buddha was meditating six years, Bodhidharma – nine. We may speed up nothing. Buddha and Bodhidharma did not happen overnight. Be patient and diligent for as Ecclesiastes said, to everything, there is a season and a time to every purpose under the heaven. This saying has a profound meaning. Just look at your past, and you surely will notice that whenever you were impatient, pushing, whenever you acted driven by emotions or disregarded your intuition, you have created problems. Meditation helps to learn that effortless experience is preferable to longing and striving.

A practice of witnessing leads to the realization of Love – a state you enter just before Freedom. Because Freedom is not an experience, witnessing and meditation are not Freedom but they are encouraging us with glimpses of Freedom and lead to Freedom.

Search among books will not help to know oneself. "For in much (Ed. human) wisdom is much grief: and he who increases knowledge increases sorrow," says Ecclesiastes, meaning spiritual knowledge.

At some point in practice, you may experience fear, apathy, grief and other negative emotions. It happens because with the conscious mind calmed, we enter our subconscious—an iceberg, made of everything we have ever experienced. Once we have entered this realm, we may as well become a witness to it. It is the most effective method of releasing because being an illusion, thoughts, and emotions of the past disintegrate as they are calmly watched.

There are several reasons why you may find group meditation helpful, especially in the beginning. A group would discipline to encourage and create collective energy that positively affects everyone in the group.

Practicing meditation, we will soon realize our mental burdens dropping away, and we are gaining access to intuitive power previously unavailable to us. There are many, who practiced meditation and obtained its fruits. Do not doubt its possibilities because of the simplicity of the method. Love, Freedom, the Truth can be found only within. Every experience can be used as a door to Love and Freedom, but meditation is a wide open door.

Classic Meditation has no goal. Goals are the property of dreamland. Goals are formulated with words, but Love and Freedom are beyond dreamland and can be only hinted with words. There is no definable bridge between dreamland and state of Love and Freedom. However, a connection can be grasped wordlessly, intuitively when you increase the time of the sessions beyond an hour☺. Thus, Samadhi is not a goal but something that happens to us spontaneously. It is somewhat similar to the state of an out-of-body experience. Meditation is a process that elevates you to loving and peaceful state.

There is no mental, emotional or physical activity in Samadhi, only existence, an inexplicable state of beingness, union with the world, and maybe with the source of creation. Samadhi entirely transforms ourselves, freeing us from the influence of all concepts. We sense this intuitively and without words.

Though thoughts and actions are absent in the state of Freedom, all positive changes caused by the power of Samadhi become functional in the state of Love that becomes our permanent state.

When Love leads us, every experience in our life becomes meditation. We are spontaneously in control without wanting to control or change anything but accepting and understanding it all. It is Enlightenment – a priceless fruit of moment-to-moment meditation called life.

Live each present moment completely and the future will take care of itself.
Fully enjoy the wonder and beauty of each instant.

Courtesy Adobe Pictures

Love and Epigenetics

We are just prisoners here of our own device
From the song *Hotel California*

Epigenetics is the key to the door of our prison. The true secret to the Wholeness, Love, and Freedom lies within our DNA; it is concealed in genes. Epigenetics is the science of studying changes in organisms caused by modification of gene expression. "Epi" means "on, upon, above," from Greek Epi. Epigenetics means above the genes.

*Live each present moment completely and the future will take care of itself.
Fully enjoy the wonder and beauty of each instant.*

In his book, *The Biology of Belief*, Dr. Lipton explains what changes our Genes. "We have cell membranes, and the DNA is inside them. The cell membranes 'read' all external signals coming from your environment and reorient the genes accordingly. It reads the external signals such as thoughts, emotions, food, motion, pollution, noise, the entire environmental input."

It means that what we eat, what we think, and how we feel controls how our genes are expressed for better or for worse.

Epigenetics proves that our body has the incredible ability to adapt and stay whole in health no matter what genetic inheritance we have. This ability to change the expression of our genes is a great gift, but we can receive it only with the realization of Love in *Transformation* or Classic Meditation. Mindfulness or any other contemporary surrogates for the Classic meditation are useless in this respect. *Transformation* provides us with direct access and ability to influence our genetic activity.

You are speaking to your genes with every thought you have. The fast-growing field of epigenetics is proving that who you are is the product of the things that happen to you in your life, which change the way your genes operate. Genes are switched on or off depending on your life experiences. What changes, is your genetic activity, meaning the hundreds of proteins, enzymes, and other chemicals that regulate your cells.

In *The Intention Experiment: Using Your Thoughts to Change Your Life and the World*, Lynne

Live each present moment completely and the future will take care of itself. Fully enjoy the wonder and beauty of each instant.

McTaggart writes: "A sizable body of research exploring the nature of consciousness, carried on for more than thirty years in prestigious scientific institutions around the world, shows that thoughts are capable of affecting everything from the simplest machines to the most complex living beings. This evidence suggests that human thoughts and intentions are an actual physical "something" with astonishing power to change our world. Every thought we have is tangible energy with the power to transform. A thought is not only a thing; thought is a thing that influences other things."

It has been well documented that directed thoughts could affect a person's own body in numerous ways. Thoughts have been shown to alter some biological processes in another person including gross motor movements, and those of the heart, eye, brain and respiratory system. Researchers have demonstrated that human intention can affect a variety of other living systems such as bacteria, mice, cats and dogs and even the direction in which fish swim. However, all this can take place when the subconscious is cleansed thus, not impending our intentions.

Having this basic understanding of Epigenetics let us come back to the subconscious and its influence. Whatever we think, feel and do necessarily is affecting our genetic makeup one way or another. However, as it was said earlier, we may think and think and think of being successful, but success would happen to someone else, why? Because whatever we think and feel is usually and easily negated by the influence of our subconscious negative past. People do not believe this because this influence is silent and invisible. We usually believe only what we see. In the spiritual world, we believe and then see results. Epigenetics is confirming what *Freedom Technique* and Lester's Wisdom books were saying all along. Indeed our ETP (Emotional Thinking Process) and the environment are affecting our genes' orientation but to effectively reorient genes in a desired manner there must be no negative subconscious influence. If there were no negative subconscious' influence, everyone would become successful just by the thought.

Our genetic inheritance also exerts a strong influence. However, Love is incomparably more powerful. It would reorient genes as desired but we have to realize Love. How many times you were getting angry, irritated, annoyed, and fearful. We exercise negative thoughts and emotions every day since our early childhood when we were taught many wrong things. Imagine how deeply embedded in the subconscious our unwanted habits. Nothing can erase it except *Transformation.* Epigenetics is scientific proof of the opportunity to influence the orientation of our genes yet; it can be accomplished only with *Transformation* or Classic meditation.

The spiritual and success industries both are flooded with *how to* books. When it comes to changes made to our genetic makeup, keep in mind, they are useless unless they offer *Transformation* or Classic meditation for only these two methods are powerful enough to banish the subconscious influence and facilitate reorientation of genes. Every other method is impotent to erase this influence.

Another way to influence our genes on a daily basis is by the past default. Chose a nice picture of you taken 20-30 years ago and make several prints large prints. Tape these prints in the visible places as a reminder. Whenever you remember it, take a good look at the picture and imagine yourself as you were at that time: healthy, happy, vital, smiling. It is your default position. Keep doing it every time you remember it.

I have incorporated this practice into my morning breathing exercise with a simple breathing tool called Voldyne 5000. You may purchase it online for about $10. This exerciser is enlarging the capacity of the lungs. With each inhalation, I would concentrate on a particular organ. Let us choose the heart. I would vividly imagine my heart saturated with a bright light and this light washing out all the impurities from and off the heart during a slow exhalation. First, after slowly breathing in, hold the air with the stomach muscles. As I am holding the air and imagining the heart saturated with the bright light, I would mentally say *True Love and the Tao revitalizing, rejuvenating, and purifying my heart by default of 1995*. Simultaneously, I would vividly imagine/picture myself looking and joyfully feeling as in my default. Then, I would slowly exhale while keeping imagining myself in 1995 and experiencing joyous feelings of the good health and wellbeing.

With the intensity and perseverance, this kind of exercise will naturally contribute to the right orientation of the genes. However, only Love would help permanently reorient genes in the appropriate manner.

Masters and mistakes

There is no such thing as perfect enlightenment. Every enlightened person, without exception, can be influenced by the elements of the environment, religious doctrines, culture with its traditions and philosophy, as well as by the genetic inheritance. In case of the enlightened person, this influence would be minimal comparing to an average human being. However, this minimal dose of the influence may cause a freeone to make mistakes.

When it comes to inner growth, an enlightened teacher is an invaluable find; an unenlightened teacher is hardly a teacher. An unenlightened teacher is teaching with his limited mind. Even a true teacher could give you only about 5% of what you need to discover Love and be free. The rest is your job. However, this 5 % would be very effective. An unenlightened teacher cannot give you this 5 % but would interpret someone else's teaching; the interpretations may have errors.

Could an unenlightened teacher teach Classic Meditation, Love, and Freedom? They could, but with a little or no help to the student; to teach efficiently a teacher must have realized Love or/and Freedom. Otherwise, the surrogates are created, something like Mindful meditation that is of a little or no help.

In education, to be to be a great teacher in any field of knowledge, the teacher must have a talent related to his field of knowledge in addition to the knowledge received in college. When there is no talent, a teacher will not be nearly as effective as the teacher who employs his talent. In the spiritual world, this talent is called Enlightenment.

Ancient teaching cannot be fully trusted unless we have original writing that we may adopt and practice. Otherwise, great caution is advised. Most ancient teachings do not have an original record. Others were transmitted verbally and what has come to us may be only a distant approximation of what the authors intended to convey.

When a teacher is not liberated, he may not be able to grasp the meaning of the message and could misinterpret it. It is why 32 Buddhist schools were created – 32 egos created their versions of the Buddha teaching instead of the one teaching – an original Buddha teaching. The Buddha teaching is simple and direct. The 32 versions are but convoluted interpretations of the simplicity.

The Secret is a useful documentary film. However, there is also an example in there of ignorance. In the film, a woman psychiatrist is warning viewers from watching the mind saying something like *there are millions of thoughts and you may go crazy trying to watch them.* This irresponsible statement would easily send an inexperienced viewer astray. The fact that this gross error is incorporated into a generally useful context of the documentary makes it even more damaging. It is just one example of an unenlightened teacher. Having no *right knowledge*, no experience, ignorance makes assumptions that confuse people.

Talentless psychologists and psychiatrists are causing more damage to their clients than good. An enlighten Master heals numberless students.

Are you a history fan? It is time to learn there is no such thing as history. It is almost all made up, twisted, and changed. History is but a fairytale, an archive where most characters are fictionalized, and the reality is altered beyond recognition. Whatever we touch in history is rarely true. It cannot be trusted. Without exception, every government is a fraud; governments are "improving" their country's history in every way they can. In the USSR, for example, the history schoolbooks were re-written four times. Most facts in every book were presented differently from what it was in the other three with many "unwanted" events deleted and the "wanted" – added. American history books are still idolizing the US presidents without any consideration given to truth. It is the same with British schools idolizing the queen and the royal family, as well as with every other government hastily weaving/creating their wishful history.

Whether modern or ancient, unless teaching offers either Classic Meditation or *Transformation*, it will not help you to the realization of Love and Freedom. Zen Masters were sometimes using quite odd methods to awake disciples, but those methods created spontaneously and are individually unique to the Masters that used them, yet, Love was the essence of their teachings.

> Therefore, the sage seeks freedom from desire.
> He does not collect precious things.
> He learns not to hold to ideas.
> He brings men back to what they have lost.

> The Tao Te Ching

An enlightened teacher is interested in you and will do his best to bring you back to what you have lost. Some teachers who are not liberated may be interested in you as much as you can bring them money. Of cause, most teachers are sincere; however, sincerity and honesty are not substituted for enlightenment. Today America is flooded with spiritual teachers. They even created a spiritual industry that set-top price for their retreats, seminars, books, and CDs. Most of them imply they are liberated. You would find the same teachers always praising each other's books although most of these books were far from the mark. However, the unenlightened

*Live each present moment completely and the future will take care of itself.
Fully enjoy the wonder and beauty of each instant.*

teacher also may help spread a good message. It is our responsibility to recognize it.

Deepak Chopra, Journalist, Medical Professional, Doctor is one of the leading spiritual minds today and a good example of how a "Master" could make a fortune just by talking. Chopra's teaching is rooted in the doctrine of reincarnation that has little to do with Love and Freedom. Fortunately, there is *The Right Knowledge* that does not support uncertainties; it does not teach fabricated concepts. *The Right Knowledge* only supports Love and Freedom.

Transformation of the subconscious past into Love eliminates any need for the entire religion with its artificial concepts, convoluted teaching of reincarnation, karma, gods, hells, and other artifacts. The Vedas, Upanishads, Bhagavad Gita and all other scriptures of all times may be set aside. The ignorant but clever even talented people composed religious scriptures filled with tails of murder, rape, and torture. To make these pieces more palpable, the writers injected jewels of wisdom in there. These uncertain, ambiguous traditions have been created to enslave and control, not to liberate. They are unnecessary in face of the *Transformation.* The only useful practices offered by the East are Yoga and Classic Meditation.

The following information regarding Chopra is from the article in The Guardian by Sue Blackmore "Deepak Chopra may be wealthy, but even he knows that's all an illusion. The guru's twisting of 'spirituality' to tell his followers that they can be rich and stay young misses the point of enlightenment."

Live each present moment completely and the future will take care of itself.
Fully enjoy the wonder and beauty of each instant.

An enlightened Master does not charge money for his teaching; he may accept donations. Mr. Chopra, a prominent figure in the New Age movement is worth $80 million that he amassed by selling his spiritual ideas at the highest price. Naturally, there are expenses involved in the creation of the books, disks, seminars, and retreats but Love dictates the lowest prices possible so that anyone would be able to afford it and... no profit made of the teachings. There should be no monetary gain made with spiritual teachings.

"Spiritual people should not be ashamed of being wealthy," Chopra declares. Mr. Chopra believes in giving, but is he giving? There are 137 wealthiest people living today who pledged 50% to 100% their fortune to charity. There is no Mr. Chopra among them.

"The effects of aging are largely preventable," says Chopra. "In moments of transcendence, when time stands still, your biological clock will stop. The spirit is that domain of our awareness where there is no time." Then why some enlightened masters, who spent years in meditation and experienced Samadhi (a moment of transcendence), aged and died at an earlier age.

It is only partially true that *in moments of transcendence when time stands still, your biological clock will stop.* However, Chopra presents it as a rule, which is enticing and misleading. If Mr. Chopra had experience of Samadhi, he would know time does not stop entirely in that state of freedom because our brain and body keep functioning. Their activity considerably slows down. Our heart may throb only a couple of times in 60 seconds, but it keeps throbbing. Neither breathing no time stops entirely in Samadhi. The effects of aging slow down indeed, but it cannot be prevented even if we sit in Samadhi for a whole year. It certainly will become preventable in the future when Love would lead the entire humanity.

Lester talked about the three levels of healing: physical, mental and spiritual, this truth has been confirmed many times. It seems a Master should have no problem instantly to his body spiritually.... Nevertheless, not every Master has this ability. Paramahansa Yogananda (1893-1952) was named Incarnation of Love. He was a wonderful teacher of Classic meditation. He died overweight at the age of 59. At the end of his life, Yogananda could hardly walk. Vivekananda, a foremost master of meditation, and the first spiritual ambassador to the US died at the age of 35.

It is true that there were Masters wholly intoxicated with God while paying no attention to their ailing body. Unfortunately, there are only a few records of such Masters. However, over centuries, these rare examples were made a rule applied to every master. An enlightened Master's life purpose is teaching Love and Freedom in selfless service to humanity. A Master would continue teaching even when he is sick. Yet, every master knows it well he would benefit people (and himself) even more and longer when his body is healthy. Then why not to heal the body and keep providing such a valuable service? Because not every enlightened person can heal his body.

There are records of the yogic experiments made in the past. A yogi descends to a 20 meters deep hole in the ground, with a small chamber at the bottom. He lies down inside the chamber, and the hole is sealed. In about 12 months, the chamber is open once more only to find yogi in perfect health. Would you want to spend a year underground to live a little longer? You would also need first to experience Samadhi to do this experiment☺

Indeed, Samadhi nearly entirely eliminates the influence of the subconscious.... When we emerge from Samadhi, some remnants of the old conditioning – subconscious influence – would still subtly influence our life. There is no teaching that is not tainted by the cultural past and present. "Masters are 100% correct!" Says Lester. It is not always true. Paramahansa Yogananda (1893-1952) was a great Master and teacher. He is also my Guru. Lester was highly respectful of Yogananda, but the Vedas and Upanishads and their concepts of gods and reincarnation greatly influenced Yogananda's teaching. Yogananda was also enforcing celibacy on Self-Realization Fellowship employees and young men who wanted to become SRF monks.

Today we know more about hormones than we knew in the fifties, as well as about consequences of the suppression. Thus, Yogananda, being a realized Master, was still limited by his convictions, which to him was not a contradiction, as Love was forever remaining the core of his teaching. It is no longer a puzzle to me how compassion, understanding, acceptance, and kindness of Love could coexist along with forced celibacy. Mental conditioning is the culprit. However, an enlightened teacher is a great find despite his mistakes.

Osho (Bhagwan Shree Rajneesh, died 1990) was a very unusual Master. He is highly respected in India and is lately was the second (after Indira Gandhi) whose entire heritage was deposited into National Archive of India. "Rajneesh's syncretic teachings emphasize the importance of meditation, awareness, love, celebration, courage, creativity, and humor – qualities that he viewed as being suppressed by adherence to static belief systems, religious tradition, and socialization. Rajneesh's teachings have had a notable impact on Western New Age thought, and their popularity has increased markedly since his death."

Wikipedia

Like most Masters of the East, Osho's teaching is rooted in reincarnation. He also implied he is the reincarnation of Buddha. On top of that, Regan and his fanatical administration did everything to discredit Osho's community in the US, eventually, deporting Osho from the country. Osho also had a bad reputation over his relationship with women. The spiritual fanatics who are erroneously asserting that no Master have sex created this gossip. Whether there are religious or spiritual, fanatics are all the same, and they are always wrong. Nevertheless, despite this negative drivel Osho had and still have a great following. He was a remarkable proponent of Love and Freedom and an outstanding teacher of Classic Meditation. When we study teaching, it is our responsibility to pick up the jewels and let go of the dross.

At the beginning of my journey, I was not able to escape the reincarnation trap. I was fascinated with the notions of reincarnation, Astral and Causal realms and beings. I wrote a novel *Gates of the Dead* taking place in those realms. It was my schooling and mostly a waste of time as if today some children feel their time in school is a waste☺. You do not need to repeat this mistake. All you need is Love that will bring everything you need with it.

When you are not sure about things like soul, an afterlife or reincarnation, etc., even when it comes from the realized Master, watch it. These ancient concepts will do no good and provide no help to you in the realization of Love and Freedom. We know there is Love, we also know there is Freedom and it is attainable. Why then to waste time on something so speculative and would give you no help. It is better to stay away from forming and adopting more concepts until we are free from the influence of all concepts. When Love is realized, you would also realize that any concept, especially religious concepts are limitations and a barrier on the path for Love is beyond all concepts.

Lester Levenson was a great Master, yet as I mentioned earlier, he said he did not want to be a teacher. However, he gave in to people's demands and agreed to Sedona Institute. Some of Lester's associates happened to be ignorant people. This Lester's mistake ended in litigation and losing the Sedona retreat. This event also made Lester abandon teaching for good.

Whatever mistakes he made, Lester also left a magnificent legacy of Love and *Transformation*. He also formulated Releasing technique that helped many to deal with negative emotions on a daily basis. Does it matter if Lester made some mistakes? It does because it makes us aware that no Master is perfect. It makes us more vigilant when we listen to a Master's talks, and more aware. When we come across some Master's mistakes all we need to do is to learn from it and let it go, keeping the jewels to ourselves☺ On several occasions Lester suggested for the students to become their teachers, ending up their search the sooner, the better.

Live each present moment completely and the future will take care of itself.
Fully enjoy the wonder and beauty of each instant.

Omar Khayyam who lived in Persia in eleven century was a well-known mathematician and astronomer. The little poems called the Rubaiyat, – songs of Love and Vine – created his world fame. Omar's poems defy time, despite the often misinterpretation of their meaning. Omar was an enlightened Master yet; he also was a worldly man. Would you less enjoy Omar's enlightening poems if you learned Omar made many mistakes, including falling in love with a beautiful young woman when he was 80? Regardless of mistakes and gossips, when we listen to the Rubaiyat with an open heart, we are uplifted and moved from our dreamland into the beautiful world of Truth.

> Oh, come with old Khayyam and leave the wise…
> To talk. One thing is certain that life flies,
> One thing is certain, and the rest is lies.
> The flower that once has blown forever dies.

Some teachers even dare to edit the Tao Te Ching. We need to discriminate so that we do not become sidetracked by the others' cleverness. To be able to do this we must learn to listen and trust our heart.

Whether another world is true or fantasy, we are forever fascinated with this mystery. The human brain consists of a great number of unknown continents and unexplored territories. The "other world" could well be a realm of the Infinite Intelligence, where every human experience is stored. That tremendous archive may contribute to the bank of Universal knowledge, to which connected that mysterious part of the human brain. Alternatively, it could be nothing.

Live each present moment completely and the future will take care of itself.
Fully enjoy the wonder and beauty of each instant.

As Andrew Carnegie once said, we are in the presence of universal law and should bow our heads in silence and obey the Judge within, asking nothing, fearing nothing, just doing our duty right along, seeking no reward here or hereafter.

We are born to live forever and we will. Today we are not aware enough to make this happen. However, in his desire to live forever and his fear of death, a man came up with countless creations of gods, deities, hells, and paradise, being sidetracked into something that has nothing to do with reality. This religious mental conditioning, a limitation, is often imposed on students. Hinduism, the oldest religion, is sometimes called the mother of religion. Does its age make it truthful? Could it be trusted? Like any other religion, it was created and enforced by the priests – Brahmins. Even like people today, Brahmins were led by their minds, not by Love. Consequently – many errors. The following exurb from the *Gates of the Dead* provides some clues on what could have happened in reality....

"When the Sun dies, our solar system will disintegrate, yet, the Vedas predicted that our Earth would die much earlier. Many thousand years past, when the wild tribes fighting each other with clubs and spears populated Europe, the Vedas provided a number with fifteen digits that is necessary to define the age of our universe in earthly years. Today, seven millenniums later, the science confirmed this number.

"By the time the Earth's evolution is completed," says Vedas, "The moon will disintegrate. It will become cosmic dust. The same destiny awaits our Earth after it fulfills its purpose. With water and other volatile matter lost, it will shrink and become attracted to another planet and humanity will begin their more developed higher astral segment of life on another planet."

No matter how clever, Brahmins were not wise people. If they were wise, India would not have millions of Untouchable living there. Even today, the Untouchable in India are treated worse than animals; they are denied all human rights. Brahmins are the ones enforcing this xenophobia.

Seven millenniums past even an enlightened person would not be able to discover *a number of fifteen digits that is necessary to define the age of our universe in earthly years*. They would not be able to come up with other modern scientific knowledge, found in Vedas even as Great Pyramid of Giza could not have been built and the scientific knowledge it contains – written by the Pharaohs and high priests of Egypt. Obviously, the more advanced visitors gave this knowledge to the Rishis. Brahmins were not able to understand this information and corrupted it by beliefs of the time.

However, by the time our Earth would begin to decay, humanity will be greatly advanced – as much as it will be able to protect the Earth from decay. Long before then, most likely around the year 4000, the ever-growing humanity will populate this ever-expanding universe and establish connections with beings living in the other universes. As the sages of the time had neither a technology nor an idea of what the universe is, they interpreted this information as humanity "will begin their more developed higher astral segment of life on another planet."

Evolution is generally developing only in a positive direction. The higher is human awareness the lesser is man's need for an artificial excitement experienced by outside sources. In about three to four hundred years from now, many forms of entertainment will disappear. Before the end of this millennium, all of it will be gone. At that time, today's "excitement" like boxing or car racing as well as any other competition will be looked upon the same way we look at the murderous fights of gladiators that were enjoyed by the "civilized" Romans two thousand years ago.

Sources of the free energy will be discovered a few hundred years earlier. There will be one government. It would become unnecessary a few hundred years after it was established. The last traces of the human ego with its negative remains will vanish with the disappearance of the government and the military. The beginning of that millennium will be the end of violence.

By the year 4000, humanity will enter a new era of self-governing. It will be led entirely by Love, as Love leads every highly advanced civilization in the other universes. It cannot be otherwise because Love is the heart of the evolution. There will be no wars, no sports, no money, no poor or rich. There will be no hospitals, doctors, and no disease as Love will guide the "new" supremely aware Human Being. A notion of security will be gone as everyone will be naturally safe. If an accident causes injury, anyone will instantly be able to heal himself. A human being will become a perfect being. Long before people would be able to correct anything contradictory to the inner growth and correct what is unnatural to the body and mind.

Every human being will naturally possess supernatural powers of omnipresence, omnipotence, etc. Transportation will disappear, as there will be nothing to transport. Man himself will cover any distance on Earth and in the Universe by means similar to what is today known as teleportation.

173

We would generate a perfect food, producing it "from thin air." We would be able nearly instantly create any structure. There will be no stars and celebrities as every human being will be a star, a god, a Master, a superhuman and "supernatural" being when compared to what we are today.

Every human being will become his and her own great universe, totally independent and self-sufficient, as well as in co-operation with all other humans, creating an Inter-Universal Oneness. This is what the Vedas interpreted as "Our humanity will be elevated to a superhuman level of the higher astral realms," where astral is, in reality, the realm of the supreme awareness and Love: a true Heaven.

In three millenniums from now, humanity will begin to live forever. It also will "raise" the dead... It will happen because of the initial design that enabled humanity's spiritual evolution leading to the realization of Love.

Was it possible for a man of the Stone Age to imagine driving his car or flying his airplane? It is as impossible for most people today to believe that human beings will be able to bring back to life their dead brethren. However, based on the speed of the progress that in the year 5000 would be racing in at least a trigonometrical progression.... as well as based on comparatively slower but steadily increasing humanity's inner growth, we can foresee human abilities being highly developed, which will enable humanity to resurrect the dead. There are other important reasons....

Eastern doctrine of reincarnation has been created based on knowledge received from the visitors. No matter how wise they have been, Rishis of the time were not able to properly digest even extremely simplified information brought to them by the visitors. However, because the "gods gave it," it was accepted but interpreted according to mental limitations of the time and adopted as such. Several millenniums later, it was "borrowed" by the Gnostics, who modified it and adopted by their views. Then it was adopted by Christianity and later – by Muslims, while it was even more "altered" in the process to fit religious doctrines of Heaven, Hell, and Resurrection. Again, the truth was not understood, especially because the meaning of consciousness, awareness, evolution, progress and many other notions was incomprehensible at the time.

As much as people were made to believe in reincarnation, afterlife, and hell, they also were made to believe in the existence of the something called Soul that was to travel in high places after death (sometimes even during life). Surprisingly, organized religions that keep fighting each other do not disagree with the Soul that is taught to be incorporeal and independent of the mind and body.

However, there is no agreement between theologies what so ever about the nature and function of the soul. According to Abrahamic religions, only human beings have immortal souls. Catholic theologian Thomas Aquinas attributed "soul" (*anima*) to all organisms but argued that only human souls are immortal, etc. Unfortunately, theology is but pseudo-science that can be described only as a soap bubble. It teaches nothing based on nothing as nearly all of its subjects is fake news that has never been confirmed by the science despite the Vatican spending millions of dollars on scientific research.

Regardless the belief that the Soul is something that is traveling to places that could have never existed, the concept of the Soul has helped to preserve some truth, which was given to people in the past. It could have been initially conveyed to Brahmins as being an incorporeal part of human mind that can project itself infinitely beyond time and space and.... maybe even to survive death. This is what reincarnation could be all about☺.

Unfortunately, there is little in common between the world of religion and spiritual world, for religious dogmas are promoting separation and violence which is contradictory to Love and oneness.

Let us take a look at the universe, as a matter of immortality is closely related to it. For such an incredibly precise Solar system as ours to come to be with such a unique planet Earth crowned with Humanity, the so-called scientific "Bang" must have been "programmed." This "programming" cannot be related in any way to today's understanding of what programming is. It could have been done only by the supremely intelligent source. We call it Infinite Intelligence.

Such creation cannot be accidental and chaotic, for chaos produces more chaos. However here we have an orderly developing magnificent system that is evolving and working throughout billions of years with unconceivable precision. Human evolution cannot be accidental either. It had to be initially "programmed." The visitors conveyed all this to people in the past.

The above is also a hypothesis but the one that is much closer to the reality than religious doctrines. Maybe Elon Musk is right saying that we live in a virtual world designed on some cosmic "computer," though there is no need for computers in the realm of Infinite Intelligence.

Our genes carry information transferred to us by the parents, grandparent, etc. This, the visitors could also have conveyed to the Rishis. Would they ever understand it?

Like all other highly advanced information, it was misunderstood and misinterpreted to fit religious doctrine of the time. The major difference between a human created God, and Infinite Intelligence is that Infinite Intelligence facilitates an entire existence without interfering in its life with punishment, rewards or otherwise. It acts without acting, as perfection "doesn't move a finger" to "create" universes but does it in ways that will be understood only in the future. What is there in common with Zeus and God? Both are created to frighten and control. Humanity is about to be done with all religious bias as Infinite Intelligence "created" this world to evolve to perfection.

In dreamland, death is viewed as negativity itself. Negativity exists only in a limited mind. Infinite Intelligence "knows" no negativity of any kind; like Love, it is beyond all concepts. If a hallucinating mind created an ill idea of Armageddon, Infinite Intelligence "created" everlasting life in Heaven called Universe. At the time of death, an entire human being's experience, no matter how insignificant or great, is "entered" in the Infinite Intelligence's "Archive" used to keep improving creation. When humanity is ripe with Love, it will access the "Archive" and use it to resurrect every human being ever walked the Earth. We are "meant" to be immortal. To be that the entire humanity has to be led exclusively by Love.

Live each present moment completely and the future will take care of itself.
Fully enjoy the wonder and beauty of each instant.

An Angel, Hurghada, Egypt

Selection

-A human being is but Infinite Intelligence made finite.

-Life is a loving journey to Happiness and Success.

-The secret of Success lies with Love.

-We choose habits as a substitute for Love and Happiness because we do not know how to find Love.

-You do not have to love anybody, anything. *Transform* your past into Love and see how your attitude and your life will change 180 degrees.

-There is no better experience for the heart than Love.

-Love knows no mental effort. Because Love is beyond effort, one who realized Love knows no stress.

-Make your computer a window into the world of Love.

-When things are done with Love, nothing is left undone.

-Love and hate cannot coexist.

-When hating, we are punishing ourselves.

-Being devoid of true Love religion is but the product of ignorance.

-To become Successful, all you need is Love

-Could Love be threatened? The mind gets frightened when Love does not lead it.

-It is nearly impossible to pinpoint a particular gene that needs to be reoriented.... Love comes to rescue.

-When realized, Love will re-arrange our genetic makeup by default.

-True Love has no religious and cultural shadows/limitations.

-In the *Transformation process,* use the word *fortunate,* instead of *lucky.*

The best thing we could do for ourselves is to help others.

-Love expels racism and slavery.

-Religion divides, Love – unites.

-Egos create wars, Love – peace.

-We do best what we truly love to do.

-Every truly beautiful thing is created with Love.

-Your subconscious is the gun loaded with the poisoned bullets of your negative past. Unless you empty this subconscious cartridge with the *Transformation*, you will suffer for the rest of your life, incessantly shot by the poisoned bullets.

-Every fight validates an ego.

-Unless you are in the state of Love, you are defenseless against the negative infection.

-Love drives away all shadows.

-The greatest and the most beneficial accomplishment in life is the realization of Love.

-Love is not justifying, judging or criticizing; it is witnessing and seeing the truth.

-Gently remind yourself to keep witnessing the mind; place the reminders (notes) in your home.

-From the time when Lester understood he could transform his negative past into Love, it took him only 30 days to realize Love.

-True Success is beneficial to its creator as well as to others. The greater is Success, the more people it will benefit.

-A success, created without Love, is a handicapped success, regardless of its size.

-Success that is not shared is forever followed by misery.

-We are never fulfilled until we realize Love.

-When Love is not yet realized we believe that our judgment is right. It is an erroneous belief because judgment is of the limited mind and in itself is an error.

-The one who is influenced by the negative past cannot see the truth because negativity, hidden in the subconscious, distorts vision. Unaware, this person would keep missing truth and.... make mistakes.

-Those who were brought up with Love and those who have discovered Love, have every opportunity at finding Happiness and (true) Success.

-There can be no Happiness without Love.

-The less acquired personality covers our unique individuality, the easier it is for us to receive intuitive advice on how to act in each circumstance.

-Not having preconceived knowledge of Love is *The Right Knowledge* and a good start. Having preconceived ideas about Love may be likened to a disease. First, realized that you are sick. Then, move towards *The Right Knowledge*, Love, and health.

-Entertainment attracts people; they enjoy it. However, *The Right Knowledge* that points to Love seems uninteresting. When you look for Love, there is nothing to see. When you realize it, its power is boundless.

-In the business world, when there is no Love, competition and connections rule a success. A true Success knows no competition.

-It is common for a business person to neglect family. When Love is the leader, both family and business benefit.

-Media pays much attention to anything but Love because an ignorant mind fears Love.

-Choosing Love means choosing Happiness and (true) Success. The moment one chooses Love is the moment when one's life and business begin thriving.

-When children are raised with Love, they would have a greater opportunity for finding Happiness and Success. It is the same with business: conducted with Love, it would bloom with (true) Success.

-When a relationship does not grow into Love, it becomes a burden. It is the same with a business. When a business is conducted in the absence of Love, it becomes a burden. The bigger is the business, the bigger the burden.

-A success without Love will bring only a temporary satisfaction and... misery.

-Love is an inner power given to us to live a life of Happiness and Success.

-Indifference is a cover for hidden negativity (greed, animosity, envy, anger, etc.). When Love is realized, indifference is gone. What left, is a loving mind.

-Witnessing is impartial. There is a difference between being indifferent and impartial. An impartial witnessing is kind, compassionate and understanding.

-Being an impartial witness, one sees through people and events.

-There is no selfishness in the desire to succeed. Every child is born to succeed. Selfishness is a refusal to share success.

-With Love, there is always the rewarding way.

Live each present moment completely and the future will take care of itself.
Fully enjoy the wonder and beauty of each instant.

-*When there is a will, there is a way* – usually the way of "pushing locomotive" – the way of ignorance. *When there is Love, there is a way* of wisdom.

-When Love enters a heart, the mind is no longer in charge; it becomes a tool. When the mind is no longer in charge, we make fewer or no mistakes because Love knows no mistakes. A mistake may happen only when we sidetrack, slip off the state of Love and choose the mind's suggestion instead.

-"How can I do what I love and be paid to support my family that requires about $100,000/year?" It can be done either by pushing or with Love that will also bestow Happiness upon you.

-Love is neither negative nor positive; it is compassionate, kind, accepting and understanding.

-Under average circumstances, the mind control is an impossible task because the subconscious silently influences the mind. To achieve control of the mind, the subconscious must be purified of the negative dross.

-Uncontrolled mind creates chaos. When Love leads the mind, it creates a life of Happiness and Success.

-When is led by Love, the mind does not need to be controlled because it is no longer a leader.

-Many problems are rooted in not loving ourselves. We must eliminate every negativity we feel about our body and mind. Our Love of the body and mind must be unconditional. Look directly into your eyes in the mirror, tell yourself "I love you (your name) unconditionally and this body as it is." Transform into Love to yourself every negative thought and feeling as they surface.

-Affirmation only can be of help when it is rooted in Love:

> "I trust the power and intelligence of Love."
> "In the universe of Love, all is whole and perfect."
> "My Life is a great adventure; I love and enjoy it's every instant."
> "I am born to succeed."
> "Love guides me to the right place at the right time..."

-You are presently successful in business, entertainment, as a student or a teacher.... However, your success did not bring you Happiness. You experience only glimpses of Happiness, which is not Happiness but a temporary satisfaction. In between these glimpses are irritation, misery, frustration, and fear – a rainbow of negative emotions that Lester calls the AGFLAP (apathy, greed, fear, lust, anger, and (false) pride).

-When you make love you are satisfied, when your partner is not responsive you are miserable; when your children obedient you are satisfied, when they do not behave you are irritated; it is the same with your employees, associates, business partners, and friends: when you are in agreement you are satisfied, when agreement is violated you are angry. Unaware, you created causes of this rollercoaster in the past, often in childhood. Now they are hiding deep in the subconscious. You cannot see these causes.

-"I used to love President Kennedy," says Val, a woman in her seventies. "When I found out what he was I lost all respect for the man; I hate him!"

"Like many others, I used to believe people get wiser when they get older. Unfortunately, this was an erroneous belief. There are many seniors in the US government, but most of them grew clever and cunning, not wiser. Whether rich or poor, famous or unknown, most people do not have enough wisdom to realize the danger of negativity. Some people even call it "human" to experience negative emotions and thoughts because they cannot imagine how to live without it.

John Kennedy was not a wise man either. Wisdom will never start a war. It will never authorize the use of Agent Orange, the deadliest of chemicals. Neither would it approve a free administering of the opium to the US soldiers in Vietnam… However, hate could take place only in the absence of Love.

-Love clears our inner vision so that we can enjoy every instant.

-We access the wisdom of the universe with the realization of Love.

-For one who realized Love there is no difference between "small" or "big" Success, it is a shared Success.

Live each present moment completely and the future will take care of itself. Fully enjoy the wonder and beauty of each instant.

-With Love, we let events take their course.

-Love is synonymous with Happiness.

-The mind can be led by the subconscious to mistakes and frustration, or Love can lead it to Happiness and Success.

-An average person would sometimes experience glimpses of Love. When Love is realized, we are immersed in the state of Love 24/7.

-With Love, we are the world.

-We did such a good job at adapting and hiding negativity; it would require an irrevocable decision and determination to "bring us back" to the reality of Love.

-Love is wisdom.

-We do not have to struggle and suffer. We are born with Love. All we need to do is to rediscover it.

-Success industry does not teach Love and (true) Success because it lacks *The Right Knowledge*. The result is disastrous as it makes millions to waste lives in chasing shadows.

-There are thousands of so-called success books like *Think and Grow Rich* by Napoleon Hill, which sold millions of copies. Save your time and money.

Live each present moment completely and the future will take care of itself. Fully enjoy the wonder and beauty of each instant.

-*The Right Knowledge* is knowledge leading to *Transformation* and Classic meditation.

-*Transformation* and Meditation move us beyond the mind's limitations and into a state of Love, then – into the realm of unencumbered peace.

-Love heals mind and body; it heals personal relationships and restores peace among nations.

-Life cannot be without problems. When Love is realized, a problem, any problem, even death will not disturb us. When the mind is Loving, our vision is clear, and we easily resolve a problem.

-Positive thinking, when it is "inborn," is a wonderful way to live. When it is not inborn, and we try to be positive, it becomes a torment. Love is the answer.

-With Love, we do not seek and hope.… we let things take their course.

-Realized Love enables total relaxation and healing.

-An idiot box is your worst enemy that literary destroying your health.

-*Transformation* of the negative past into Love is a skill. Like any other skill, it can be learned. It is learned in practice.

-When Love leads, people follow.

Live each present moment completely and the future will take care of itself.
Fully enjoy the wonder and beauty of each instant.

-Every moment must be intensely felt and fully enjoyed.

-Every success is created with confidence and self-esteem. However, if not rooted in Love, a success will work against us with stress, anxiety, and fear.

-Love knows no holiness, morality or justice; it knows kindness, Happiness, and Success.

-Guilt has no real purpose, yet people are holding on to guilt throughout their lives.... A man was captured by the enemy and tortured to cooperation. After the war, he became a politician. However, that guilt created by his capture did not dissolve by itself; it made the man a saber-rattler. His position gives him a momentary satisfaction in destroying others yet, guilt and hate have turned his life into an unhappy journey.

-When she was young, a woman was too busy with her boyfriend and cared little for her son. She lost her child through negligence. 40 years later, she still cannot forgive herself. Her feeling of guilt made her irritable and angry, causing her to ruin relationships and lose jobs. She believes her guilt is a deserved punishment, that she has no right to be happy. Love knows no guilt and no punishment.

- With Love, Success is always true.

-Our future is shaped by the four elements: thinking/imagination, emotions, environment and subconscious influence. The subconscious influence is hidden from view.

- Without Love, we are hardly surviving in our dreamland.

-When ill, irritation and anger contribute to illness; Love heals.

-If you were repeatedly told by your parents, "you are no good" it could have resulted in criticizing and blaming yourself, in procrastination and laziness, and in an inferiority complex. Love will cure you.

- You may repeat it an infinite number of times: "The past has no power over me" yet, it will keep exerting great influence over your every decision because just by repeating the words it is impossible to eradicate hidden causes. Affirmation, when rooted in Love, can be only a helpful aid to *Transformation,* no more than that.

-If releasing technique can be compared to remodeling an apartment, *Transformation* can be likened to moving from the apartment to the beautiful house.

-Love gets her way without pushing and striving.

-Love loves a smile.

-Love does not take sides.

-With Love, we are content and happy to be ourselves.

Live each present moment completely and the future will take care of itself. Fully enjoy the wonder and beauty of each instant.

-Love banishes fear, even the fear of death.

-With Love, you are forever secure and safe.

-The best diet is a mental diet.

-The biggest problem is the same for all people: the absence of Love.

-Love is like a well; it is inexhaustible.

-With the realization of Love, we do not crave money and security; we always have what we need.

-An incredible intelligence within us can be expressed in full only with the power of Love. Then, is president Obama incredibly intelligent? Obama and alike politicians are but the expression of the utter clever ignorance.

-Love is effortlessly nourishing all things.

-Love has all the answers.

-Love is the answer.

-There are no impediments to the realization of Love except conditioning and resistance created by our negative past. We need to accept and transform it into loving ourselves.

-To love yourself means <u>always</u> to be lovingly supportive of yourself.

-Once you come to love yourself, you will forever enjoy this affair.

-It is hard to correct problems while having the biggest problem of all: the absence of Love.

-Everything falls into place when Love is our guide.

-Always, begin your day with gratitude for everyone and everything you have.

-The absence of Love is the only cause of inequality.

-The absence of Love means the presence of ignorance.

-When negativity is gone, mind falls quiet. When the mind is naturally at ease, the body easily takes care of itself.

-When Love is realized, we are in the flow, enjoying each present moment, and letting the future to take care of itself.

-Craving Love realization is an obstacle as it emphasizes the lack of realization. Instead, there should be a conviction that realization is at hand.

-If you still doubt Love's supreme power that brings Happiness and Success, do your simple research. You will learn that every human problem is rooted in the absence of Love. What does the following tell you: Seventy-five percent of all American children knew no Love in their childhood? How many politicians are honest and sincere?

Only a few. The underlying reason is an unhappy upbringing, the absence of Love. As a rule, the wrongdoers had no love in their childhood, and there is no Love present in their adult life. Examine your life to learn that mistakes you made were made because the mind, not Love guided you.

-Happiness and Success are everyone's birthright.

-Those who are not kind, honest and sincere have been mentally conditioned this way in the absence of Love.

-With Love, you are the lion that moves alone: you are independent of the others' opinions and judgments. You have everything you need when you need it. You know what is necessary for you to know in a life of Happiness and Success.

-Your irritability is rooted in your negative past.

-The trinity is Mind, Body, and Love, where Love leads the Mind.

-Ignorance is pushing, Love – understanding and accepting.

-In the heat of arguing, suddenly, stop arguing and remember yourself. At this moment you are Free.

-It is not the length but the quality of a life that counts.

-The quality of life is characterized <u>only</u> by the presence of Love.

-When you are open to Love, you are one with Love.

-Talent is not the true heart of Success, Love is.

-Success without Love is like a red color for a bull: it keeps aggravating the successful by reminding of the absence of Happiness.

-The life's moment not enjoyed is the moment lost. Fully enjoy the wonder and beauty of each instant.

-Love has no attachments.

-With Love, we see with inner vision.

-When Love is realized, we stop the following anyone, even the Master, as we are threading our unique path leading to Freedom.

-Love rejects no one.

-When we unconditionally accept the world, we are in Love.

-Do you still want to improve the world?

-This world is designed to evolve to perfection.

-Weapons are the tools of fools.

-Love knows no enemy.

-Undisturbed inner peace is the Love's chief value.

-Religious prayer was designed to control your inner world from outside. Learn to control your outer word from inside.

-Infinite Intelligence is there for everyone to use. Begin with the Love-realization, and you will be guided to the next step.

-When there is no true Love, people create religions, deities, and Gods.

-Releasing method is quite useful to control our emotional states in daily life. To find life-lasting Happiness we need to realize Love.

-Change yourself, and you have changed the world.

-Love is harmony. It is also, fun, game, and joy.

-Love brings forth the best of you.

-There is a mind of Love and.... nothing else.

-Every belief is a limitation. Do not believe in Love, be Love.

Live each present moment completely and the future will take care of itself.
Fully enjoy the wonder and beauty of each instant.

-A principle is a limitation. Life and nature are bereft of principles.

-Do not waste your life on watching the news for it is forever fake.

-Enlightenment does not entirely eliminate the influence of the past hidden in the subconscious.

-A harmful negative event will not harm you when Love leads you.

-Creators of the violent entertainment and pornography are ignorant people, a humanity's waste.

-Mental Conditioning and Resistance programs make truth hard to accept.

-Watching the mind brings the realization of the present moment.

-When we let things happen, everything happens promptly.

-A drop of the sea contains the entire sea. Each present moment contains all life that includes your life.

-When Love is realized, we benefit humanity incomparably more than any world-famous personality.

-For Lester's quotes on Love, please, see books *Wisdom by Lester.*

Live each present moment completely and the future will take care of itself.
Fully enjoy the wonder and beauty of each instant.

Bibliography

Andrew Carnegie *Autobiography*

Andrew Carnegie *The Gospel of Wealth*

Dr. Jack Lee Rosenberg *Body, Self, Soul and Sustaining Integration*

Grabovoi Grigori *Concentration Methods*

Lao Tsu, *Tao Te Ching*, Vintage Books, 1972

Levenson, Lester, *The Final Step to Freedom* (in public domain)

Lloyd, Virginia, *Choose Freedom*, Freedom Publications, Phoenix, Arizona, 1983

Napoleon Hill, *The Law of Success*

Price, A. & Wong Mou-Lam, *The Sutra of Hui Neng*, Hyperion Press, Inc., Westport, Connecticut, 1973

Red Pine, translator, *Zen Teaching of Bodhidharma*, North Point Press, San Francisco, 1989

Vivekananda, Swami, *The Yoga and Other Works*, Ramakrishna-Vivekananda Center, New York, 1996

Wood, Ernest, *Zen Dictionary*, Charles E Tuttle Company, Tokyo, Japan, 1988

Live each present moment completely and the future will take care of itself.
Fully enjoy the wonder and beauty of each instant.

About the Author

Yuri Spilny was born in Vladivostok, Russia. His life has been varied and unusual. After six years in Navy School, he decided it was not for him. "When awakening for duty, I was hit with this," he says, "Now walk out of here!" And I left the School just three months before graduation." He went to Moscow Film School and began a successful career as a documentary filmmaker. Traveling the world, he produced over 70 documentary films on a wide variety of subjects. He lectured at the University of Economics and Moscow State University on Awareness, Responsibility, and Freedom. In North America, he studied religious philosophies, practiced meditation. "I always knew," he says, "that my destiny was to write," and he wrote *The Incredible Adventures of Kitto*, beautifully illustrated trilogy of fairytales emphasizing to young readers "every child is born to succeed." His recent books are *Gates of the Dead,* a spiritual novel; *Freedom Technique: Path to Awareness and Love* and *The Lion Moves Alone* (see: Yuri Spilny at Amazon.com/books). Yuri lives in Sequoia National Forest, California.   yuri@bookstoenjoy.com

Live each present moment completely and the future will take care of itself.
Fully enjoy the wonder and beauty of each instant.

Other books by the author

"This book is for your heart... In this book, Yuri makes you ask yourself.... Can I learn to trust something more than my mind? Like Alice in Wonderland and her steps through the mirror, am I so close and still not seeing: 'IT' has been within me all the time? Why do I insist on hanging on to my mind's guidance when it knows so little about Life? Can I quiet my mind long enough to give my heart the first say in the rest of my life's journey?

"I have found this to be a priceless exercise. And I am now embracing this journey that I have always been on but for the first time with an embracing of no limits to the volume of love I can contain. I've turned the mirror around, and I see my inner self."

Jill Sloan, Kernville, CA

Live each present moment completely and the future will take care of itself. Fully enjoy the wonder and beauty of each instant.

Freedom Technique: Path to Awareness and Love with Autobiography by Lester Levenson

Kindle: http://www.amazon.com/kindle/dp/B006XZZM0E

Paperback: https://www.createspace.com/3694994

First, comes desire, it is followed by hope, by disappointment and suffering; then comes search. Search discovers Love. With Love comes the simplicity of being in the "now" and joy that melts down desires. The mind is educated when your entire past is transformed into Love. When it happens, Love becomes the leader, and the educated, aware mind follows the Love's intuitive lead.

Kindle: http://www.amazon.com/dp/B00GEKWLQQ

Paperback: https://www.createspace.com/4298483

Live each present moment completely and the future will take care of itself.
Fully enjoy the wonder and beauty of each instant.

Lester's wisdom in three volumes.

You can have, be, and do whatever you will or desire. The only thing stopping you is the accumulation of negative thoughts and feelings, which you are subconsciously holding. Remove these, and you remove the blocks to your accomplishing whatever you wish in life. Remove these, and you will find love, happiness, and joy beyond your wildest dreams. Remove these, and you are Free.

Love is absolutely necessary ingredient on the path. To get full Realization, we must increase our love until it is complete.

Lester Levenson

Lester's Wisdom in three volumes available in Kindle format and paperback.

Live each present moment completely and the future will take care of itself.
Fully enjoy the wonder and beauty of each instant.

The Incredible Adventures of Kitto

Set of three books (8.5"x 11") with over 80 original illustrations in **Full Color**

A set of three original books is available at www.bookstoenjoy.com

E-books, as well as softcover books, are available at Amazon.com

Live each present moment completely and the future will take care of itself.
Fully enjoy the wonder and beauty of each instant.

THE MIDWEST BOOK REVIEW
The Children's Bookwatch
An official Newsletter of
The Midwest Book Review
http://www.execpc.com/~mbr/bookwatch/

The Incredible Adventures of Kitto
Yuri Spilny
Bookstoenjoy.com
HC1, Box 106, Kernville, CA 93238
yuri@bookstoenjoy.com

Beautifully illustrated with more than eighty original watercolors by Anna and Nada Balzhak, "The Incredible Adventures of Kitto" is a wondrous trilogy of fairytale stories that emphasize to their young readers "every child is born to succeed."

Sorceress's Spell (1-892316-00-5) follows ten-year-old Kitto as he incurs the wrath of the wicked Milady. Escaping Milady's powers via a flying dragon and aided by the good Fairy Sambhava, Kitto creates four magical toys who become Kitto's best friends. The Toynapers (01-3) finds Kitto bringing his toys to participate in The Greatest Toy Show on Earth, where Princess Daisy falls in love with them, and her father makes Kitto his royal toy master -- only to see Kitto end up falsely accused of a terrible crime, convicted and imprisoned. River of Fire (02-1) begins with a breathtaking escape for now blind Kitto through the services of his good friend, the flying dragon. Aided by Fairy Sambhava once again, Kitto and his toys travel to the enchanted River of Fire. Together they encounter and overcome great dangers. Eventually, they reach the Pearl Palace of a terrible wizard and obtain a very special treasure.

A highly recommended fairytale trilogy.

James A. Cox, Editor-in-Chief.

"...Their love was not of this world. They knew nothing except great love for each other. It was all they had, and they didn't want anything else." The Magician fell silent, looking at distant mountains veiled in the blue mist of a dying day. From that far-away mountain country or maybe from that ancient realm where unearthly love had once bloomed, a flock of birds flew in, as if greeting the Magician....

*Live each present moment completely and the future will take care of itself.
Fully enjoy the wonder and beauty of each instant.*

... A timeless, enlightening adventure, a flight from grief in search of happiness.

This story is spun by a loving and creative writer, but it is the subject of the story – the meaning of love, life and death – and its treatment that set the book apart. *Gates of the Dead* has importance both timely and timeless and contains much practical wisdom that can be taken at many levels depending on the reader's receptivity. As a contribution to the subject of Love, it is unique among the books on the subject.

> Prof. Olga Volkogonova, Department of Philosophy of Science. Moscow State University

This story offers greater insight into the little voice inside all of us that speaks directly to and through our hearts. There are no accidents to love. And fleeting as it may feel at times when bound to this earth's rules, it is truly limitless on the other side.

.   Jill Sloan, Kernville, California

Paperback: https://www.createspace.com/4416121

Also available on Kindle at Amazon.com

205

99639742R00113

Made in the USA
Columbia, SC
11 July 2018